First World War
and Army of Occupation
War Diary
France, Belgium and Germany

74 (YEOMANRY) DIVISION
230 Infantry Brigade
Buffs (East Kent Regiment)
10th Battalion
1 May 1918 - 1 May 1919

WO95/3153/2

The Naval & Military Press Ltd
www.nmarchive.com
Published in association with The National Archives

Published by

The Naval & Military Press Ltd

Unit 10 Ridgewood Industrial Park,

Uckfield, East Sussex,

TN22 5QE England

Tel: +44 (0) 1825 749494

www.naval-military-press.com

www.nmarchive.com

This diary has been reprinted in facsimile from the original. Any imperfections are inevitably reproduced and the quality may fall short of modern type and cartographic standards.

© **Crown Copyright**
Images reproduced by permission of The National Archives, London, England, 2015.

Contents

Document type	Place/Title	Date From	Date To
Heading	WO95/3153/2 10 Battalion East Kent Regiment (Buffs)		
Heading	74th Division 230th Infy Bde 10th Bn East Kent Regt (The Buffs) 1918 May-1919 May		
War Diary		01/05/1918	31/05/1918
Miscellaneous	Summary For The Month of May		
War Diary		01/06/1918	30/06/1918
Miscellaneous	Summary 1st-30th June 1918		
War Diary		01/07/1918	31/08/1918
Miscellaneous	Summary 1st-31st August 1918		
War Diary		02/09/1918	31/10/1918
War Diary	Hertain	01/11/1918	09/11/1918
War Diary	Tournai	09/11/1918	14/11/1918
War Diary	Herquegies	15/11/1918	18/11/1918
War Diary	Barry	19/11/1918	16/12/1918
War Diary	Thollebeek	17/12/1918	31/12/1918
War Diary	Thollembeek Belgium	01/01/1919	24/01/1919
War Diary	Brussels	25/01/1919	28/01/1919
War Diary	Thollembeek	29/01/1919	31/01/1919
Miscellaneous	Summary from 1st to 31st Jan 1919		
War Diary	Thollembeek Belgium	01/02/1919	08/02/1919
War Diary	Vollezeel Belgium	08/02/1919	26/02/1919
War Diary	Frammont Belgium	27/02/1919	28/02/1919
War Diary	Grammont	01/03/1919	01/05/1919

WO/95/3153/2

10 Battalion East Kent Regiment (Buffs)

74TH DIVISION
230TH INFY BDE

10TH BN EAST KENT REGT
(THE BUFFS)
~~1918 MAY - DEC 1918~~
~~JAN 1919~~

1918 MAY —— 1919 MAY

WAR DIARY or INTELLIGENCE SUMMARY.

Army Form C. 2118.

(Erase heading not required.)

Place	Date	Hour	Summary of Events and Information	Remarks and references to Appendices
May 1918	1st		W/S & Tonning Bn'd of Convoy Put to Sea 2017 arrived at Mudros 2 of whom went (Sick) off the Strength on being sent ashore.	
	2nd		At Sea (on board H.T. MALWA) enr to Italy	
	3rd		" " "	
	4th		" " "	
	5th		" " "	
	6th		" " "	
	7th		Arrived at Marseilles Awaiting Train (MARSEILLES) Rt. Attaching 1st O.K. 1st Battalion Strength Leaving Shrub to Shrub Besides Battalion went into camp at No 12 Camp.	
	8th		Son to Stagnant River off Tryst (& Run Parlours) to England	
			Taken over Strength	
	9th		Entrained at MARSEILLES	
	10th		On Road train	
	11th		Arrived att'd training Battn (NOVELLES) Arrived at held at FOREST L'ABBAYE	
	12th		" "	
	13th		Stor to acquired Strength off Strength	
	13th		Transport & Beyers went forward to Regt Lodge transport	
	14th		W. CR to PLOUGEC	

WAR DIARY or INTELLIGENCE SUMMARY

Army Form C. 2118.

Place	Date	Hour	Summary of Events and Information	Remarks and references to Appendices
May/16	15		60R to Hospital Shock off Strength	
	16		10R transferred to R.E. Shock off Strength, R1 OR to Hospital Shock off Strength. Lt. R.H. ATKINSON 1 BOR allowed Gas Course	
			NOUVION	
	17		20R to Hospital Shock off Strength	
	18		3 OR proceeded on time expired leave to ENGLAND	
			20 OR to Hospital Shock off Strength	
	19		2 OR from " " taken on "	
			3 OR " " Shock off "	
	20		Lt. R.H. ATKINSON & 9 OR to Hospital Shock off Strength	
	21		3 OR to Hospital Shock off Strength	
			10 OR admitted attached 1/8 Lg. Scottish & 1 OR to Hospital Shock off Strength	
	30		Battalion moved to BUNEVILLE went into Billets	
			7 OR to Hospital Shock off Strength	
	28		all BUNEVILLE 90R to Hospital Shock off Strength	
	29		" "	

Capt. J.L. HERON, O.C. attached to Eng. and On Bn. Wassernall Camp

WAR DIARY
INTELLIGENCE SUMMARY

Army Form C. 2118.

Place	Date	Hour	Summary of Events and Information	Remarks and references to Appendices
May 1918	24th (Cont)		4 OR on line Escorted leave check off strength. 3 OR to 7th Divisional HQ for Traffic Control Duty struck off Strength wd.	
	25th		Battalion moved to IZEL-LEZ-HAMEAU went into Billets 2 Lieut F.S. DOWNIE was posted to Battalion & Officer wd. 1 OR to Hospital Struck off Strength. Lieut C.J.G. SWAINSON & 2nd Lieut C.E. COURT joined the Battalion from reinforcement Camp & were taken on Strength wd. Evans taken on Strength wd. 1 OR joined from reinforcement camp & 1 OR from Hospital taken on Strength wd.	
	27th		1 OR to Hospital Struck off Strength. Lt. R.A. NAPIER rejoined from reinforcement camp 1 OR from L.I. M.B. were taken on Strength wd.	
	28th		Battalion was inspected by G.O.C. 7th Division Lt. H.O.B. Barnard proceeded on Compassionate leave to England & 2 OR on line Escorted leave to England. 3 OR to Hospital Struck off Strength wd.	
	29th		6 OR to Hospital Struck off Strength. Lieut H.Y.B. THORNTON from 2nd R.E.D.M.T. & Lieut C.E. Smith from 3rd The Buffs joined the Battalion from U.K. wd. 2/Lt. proceeded on line Escorted leave to England 1 OR to Hospital struck off the Strength. 1 OR from Hospital taken on Strength wd.	

WAR DIARY
INTELLIGENCE SUMMARY.

Place	Date	Hour	Summary of Events and Information	Remarks and references to Appendices
May 1918	29th		Lieut. Col. THE LORD SACKVILLE. T.D. received instructions to proceed to the British mission at French G.H.Q. from duty as Liaison Officer with	
	30th		Egyptian S.O.R. to 4th/4th Strength (OR from Hospital not from reinforcements taken on strength. ed.	
	31st		2 O.R. to Hospital. Struck off strength on sinks C.B. WENTWORTH STANLEY. S/S TURNPENNY. F.S. DOWNS. L.H.S. DURSTON, & Lieut. & Qm. A.KINGSFORD, & 13 OR. proceeded on leave to the U.K. ret.	

Sackville
Lt Col
Cmdg. (E. & W. KENT YEO) BN THE BUFFS

Summary
For the month of May. 1st–31st

1. Administrative

During the course of the month Drafts of 3 officers (Lieut A/S Thornton & Lieuts Smith CE & Cavit CA.) & 10 Rank joined the Battalion for duty & were taken on the Strength

The following appointments were made:-
Lieut JS Downs appointed Batt. Sig. Officer
" C.W. Hickson " " Bombing "
" " " " " L. Gun "

The following Courses were attended:-
1 officer & 6 OR.   Gas Course   at NOUVION
1 OR   "   AGNES-LES-DUISANS
2 officers & 8 OR   Anti aircraft mounting
                    for Lewis Guns   IZEL-LEZ-HAMEAU
1 officer & 6 OR   Bayonet fighting Course PONT NOILE

2. Discipline
The general Discipline of the Battalion continued good throughout the period

3. Health. The number of men reporting sick on arrival at the new Theatre of Operations was largely increased. The majority of cases being Influenza colds & Pirexia
One case of Infectious Disease was reported. measles.

4. Ordnance Services Good
5. Supply   "   "
6. Transport   "   "

7. Operations & Training
On the 1st of the month the Battalion sailed from ALEXANDRIA on board Ship 'C' (H.M.T. MALWA) and after a voyage of 6 days, arrived at the Port of Disembarkation (MARSEILLES). The voyage itself was quite devoid of incident. A certain amount of Physical Training & Gas Training was undergone whilst on board Ship, & where possible Lewis Gun Training was undertaken. After a stay of 2 days at Rest Camp (MARSEILLES) the Battalion proceeded North by train and arrived at detraining point

7. Operations & Training (Cont'd).
(NOYELLES) on 11th May and marched into Billets at FOREST L'ABBAYE, a distance of about 5 miles

Training was immediately started, with very special reference to Protection against Gas. Courses were started for Lewis Gunners, Signallers Sniper Scouts, and considerable attention was paid to Bayonet fighting

On the 22nd of the month the Battalion moved to BUNEVILLE and went into Billets, where training was continued

On the 25th the Battalion again moved and marched to IZEL LEZ HAMEAU and went into Billets

On 28th The Battalion was Inspected by G.O.C. 74 Division

Courses.

Gas.	1 off 6 OR at.	NOUVION
do	1 OR "	AGNES LES DUISANS
Anti Aircraft mounting for Lewis Guns.	2 off 8 OR "	IZEL LEZ HAMEAU
Bayonet fighting.	1 off 5 OR "	PONT HUILE

Sackville.
Lt Col
Cmdg (E. & W. KENT YEO) The BUFFS

Army Form C. 2118.

10th Bn. The R.H.[?]/...

VOL 3   JUNE 1918

WAR DIARY
or
INTELLIGENCE SUMMARY.
(Erase heading not required.)

Place	Date	Hour	Summary of Events and Information	Remarks and references to Appendices
June 1918	1st		Lieut. Col. the LORD SACKVILLE T.D. left the Battalion to take up duty with the British Military Mission, at G.Q.G. French Army, as Liaison Officer. Major Cuthbertson assumed command of the Battalion.	
			2 O.R. to Hospital. Struck off strength.	
	2nd		4 " " " " "	
			1 " from " taken on	
			2 " to " struck off	
	3rd		9 O.R. proceeded on short leave to England	
			1 " June Eschwege[?] " "	
			1 " " Draft. 4 O.R. from Hospital taken on the strength	
	4th		6 " to Hospital Struck off strength	
			1 " from 14th Divisional Signal Company taken on strength	
	5th		1 " proceeded on Gas Course at ACHNES LES DUISANS[?]	
	6th		1 " to Hospital Struck off strength	
			1 " to " " "	
	7th		5 " " " taken on	
			2 " from " "	
	8th		1 " to " Struck off	

WAR DIARY
or
INTELLIGENCE SUMMARY.
(Erase heading not required.)

Army Form C. 2118.

Place	Date	Hour	Summary of Events and Information	Remarks and references to Appendices
June 1918	9th		30. OR to Hospital. Struck off strength + 8 OR from Hospital taken on.	
			22 OR proceeded to AUBIN ST WAAST on week's musketry course.	
	10th		2 " to Hospital struck off strength. 40R from hospital taken on. 9 " proceed on short leave to England.	
	11th		3 " to Hospital struck off strength. 2 OR joined as Chaplain taken on. 4S OR returned from 10 Infantry Base there taken on strength.	
	12th		3 OR to Hospital struck off strength. 2 OR from Hospital taken on strength. 20R succeeded to A.P.M. 7th Division for specific combat duty.	
	13th		There struck off strength. 4 OR to Hospital struck off strength. Capt. J.H. FRIEND & 10 OR rejoined from leave to England.	
	14th		8 " to Hospital struck off strength	
	15th		3 " " " " " " "	
	16th		5 " from Bde. MO + 23 OR LTMB rejoined for duty taken on.	
			taken on strength.	
	17th		9 OR proceeded on leave to England. Lts. C.S.B WENTWORTH-STANLEY, F.S. DOWNS, H.S. DURSTON, S.B. TURNPENNY, Hon. Lt. & Qm. A. KINGSFORD 4 OR returned from leave to England.	

WAR DIARY
or
INTELLIGENCE SUMMARY

Army Form C. 2118.

Place	Date	Hour	Summary of Events and Information	Remarks and references to Appendices
June 1918	17th		The Rev. Roughly C.F. was attached to the Battalion for duty.	
	16th		5 O.R. to Hospital. Struck off strength. 4 I.O.R.'s & 1 Sgt. R.A.M.C. Struck off strength. 4 O.R. rejoined from leave to England.	
			19 O.R. joined Battalion as a draft from England (these taken on strength)	
	18th		6 O.R. to Hospital. Struck off strength. Lt. R.H. ATKINSON rejoined from Hospital (taken on strength). 1 O.R. proceeded on short leave to England	
	20th		2 O.R. to Hospital. Struck off strength. 1 O.R. from " " taken on "	
	21st		4 O.R. to Hospital. Struck off strength. 1 O.R. to A.P.M. 7th R.K. Division. Struck off strength. 3 O.R. from Hospital taken on strength. 2nd Lt. SILLEEK & Lt. R.H. ATKINSON proceeded on leave to ENGLAND & 10 O.R. proceeded on leave to ENGLAND. 6 O.R. returned from leave to England.	
	22nd		6 O.R. proceeded to England for a Cadet course (names which off strength) 5 O.R. to Hospital. Struck off strength. 5 O.R. proceeded to England on Cadet Course (names Struck off strength). 4 O.R. returned to England from leave to England.	
			1 O.R. proceeded on leave to England	

Army Form C. 2118.

WAR DIARY
or
INTELLIGENCE SUMMARY.
(Erase heading not required)

Instructions regarding War Diaries and Intelligence Summaries are contained in F.S. Regs., Part II. and the Staff Manual respectively. Title pages will be prepared in manuscript.

Place	Date	Hour	Summary of Events and Information	Remarks and references to Appendices
June 16	23rd		2 OR to Hospital, struck off strength. 1 OR from Hospital taken on. Major W.O. LITTLE joined the Battalion on duty, was taken on strength of the Command. Continued training.	
	24		1 OR to Hospital struck off strength. 1 OR proceed to ENGLAND on a cadet course, was struck off strength. Capt. E. TRICKERY (Army) & Lt. THE HON. R.M.T. HESIGER†JOR proceed on 14 days leave to ENGLAND. 3 OR from Hospital. 1 OR as Duty. 1 OR from Hospital to ENGLAND joined the Battalion & were taken on strength.	
	25th		The Battalion moved by rail & road route into billets at ENGUNN	
			LES MINES. 9 OR to Hospital struck off strength 10 OR from Hospital taken on.	
	26th		1 OR to Hospital, struck off strength.	
	27th		3 OR to " " " " " 2 OR from Hospital returns struck on.	
	28		3 OR to " " " " " 1 OR proceed on leave to England.	
	29		2 OR to " " " " " " " " " "	
	30		1 OR " " " " " " " " " "	

C H Baleton
Major
Comdg 1st Batt The Buffs.

Summary.
1st – 30th June 1918.

1. Administrative

During the Course of the month 2 officers joined the Battalion. Major W.O. LITTLE* & The Rev A. ROUGHLY. C.F.   *Westmorland & Cumberland Yeo'y

Lt. Col. THE LORD SACKVILLE left the Battalion to take up duty with the British Military Mission at G.Q.G. French Army as Liaison Officer. Major C.H. Balston assumed command of the Battalion.

2 Drafts of O.R. joined the Battalion from England one of 19 & the other of 22. Their General Physique was good & their average period of service 3 years & 2 years respectively.

The following Courses were attended:

8 O.R.	L.T.M.B Course	230th Bde. LTMB
1 O.R.	Gas	AGNES-LES-DUISANS
4 O.R.	Signalling	230th Bde HQ
1 O.R.	P. & B.T Course	HARDELOT PLAGE
1 O.R.	Carrier Pigeons	Corps HQ.
3 O.R.	do.	CONTES
1 Officer	General	AUBIN ST VAAST
~~1~~	~~Lewis Gun~~	
2 O.R.	General Course	AUBIN ST VAAST
1 O.R.	Lewis Gun	" "

2. Discipline

The discipline of the Battalion continued Good throughout the period.

Summary (Cont'd)

3. **Health**
There have been a large number of men reporting sick, Influenza Colds & Pyrixia being still prevalent. But the general health of the Battalion has been, on the whole good. No cases of infectious deseases were reported.

4. **Ordnance Services** — Good
5. **Supply Services** — Good
6. **Transport Services** — Good
7. **Operations & Training**

During the month the Battalion was placed on G.H.Q. Reserve and was at 24 hours notice to move. For a short period this was reduced to 9 hours but was subsequently put back to 24 hours.

On the 25th the Battalion moved, partly by road & partly by rail to another area further north and went into billets at ENQUIN-LES-MINES. The Battalion continued to form part of G.H.Q Reserve but was placed at 4 hours notice to move. During the whole month, vigorous training was continued, & opportunities were afforded for practicing the attack in conjunction with Tanks.

C H Balston
Major
Cmdg. 1/oo Batt. The Buffs

WAR DIARY
or
INTELLIGENCE SUMMARY.

Army Form C. 2118.

10 Buffs
JULY 1914

Place	Date	Hour	Summary of Events and Information	Remarks and references to Appendices
July 1918.	1st		3 OR to Hospital Struck off Strength. 8 OR from Hospital taken on strength.	
	2nd		Lt. J.R.S. AYLWARD. M.C. + 7 OR proceeded on short Leave to ENGLAND. 10 OR to Hospital. Struck off strength. 4 OR from Hospital taken on strength.	
	3rd		2 OR to Hospital struck off strength. 5 OR from hospital taken on strength. Lt. C.S. DOWNING rejoined the Battalion from Hospital. 11 OR joined the Battalion as a Draft. were taken on strength from ENGLAND	
	4th		4 OR to Hospital struck off strength. 1 OR from hospital taken on strength. 12 OR joined the Battalion as a Draft. were taken on strength.	
	5th		1 OR from Hospital taken on strength.	
	6th		9 OR proceeded on short Leave to ENGLAND. 5 OR from Hospital taken on strength. Lieut. C.F.G. SWAINSON. 2/4 C/FCOUNT 4 OR proceed on Courses of Instruction.	
	7th		3 OR returned from (APPU) 74th Division taken on strength. 2 OR from hospital taken on strength. 3 OR to Hospital struck off strength to 1 OR from Hospital struck off strength. 3 OR from Hospital taken on	

WAR DIARY
or
INTELLIGENCE SUMMARY.

(Erase heading not required.)

Army Form C. 2118.

Place	Date	Hour	Summary of Events and Information	Remarks and references to Appendices
July.18	10th		Battalion moved into Divisional Reserve and proceeded by motor lorries to HAM EN ARTOIS. Was killed for the night. Capt A/major. C.H. BALSTON was appointed Lieut Col. which by command of the Battalion (16-6-18). Capt J.I.H. FRIEND was appointed A/major which employed on the H.Q. of an Infantry Battalion & opened ... in command of his Battalion (16-6-18) ETEAMS proceeded to the Divisional neighbors camp at WITTERNESS	
	11th		Battalion moved into Brigade Reserve to the front line & proceeded to LA PIERRIERE relieving the 2/R.WARWICK REGT. 2.Lieut. into Bivk. 10R from hospital taken on strength. 2Lt J.W. MANN 1st Batt "Ye Buffs") joined as a draft from ENGLAND was taken on strength. Lt The Hon P.M. THESIGER + Capt P.VICKERY (RAMC attached) returned from leave to ENGLAND	
	12th		2.OR to hospital struck off strength. Capt. CRAIB (RAMC attached) returned to 2/30th Field Ambulance	
	13th		1.OR to Hospital struck off strength. 10R to ENGLAND on a Catt. Course struck off strength.	
	14th		2.Lt W.C. GURR & 3.OR returned from tour of duty at HEZECQUES	

WAR DIARY
INTELLIGENCE SUMMARY

Place	Date	Hour	Summary of Events and Information	Remarks and references to Appendices
July/18	15th		1 OR from Hospital Taken on strength	
	16th		10 OR proceeded to England on a Cadet Course was struck off strength 1 OR to Hospital struck off strength. 2 OR Killed 1 OR wounded (1 of whom subsequently died) whilst on a working party.	
	17th		1 OR to Hospital struck off strength.	
	18th		3 OR to Hospital struck off strength. 9 OR from Hospital taken on strength.	
	19th		2 OR from 10th Batt. the Buffs joined as a Draft taken on strength. Lieut. JAS. AYLWARD M.C. rejoined from Leave to UK 1 OR from Hospital taken on strength. Lieut. W.C. GURR. proceeded on to 2 days Leave to UK.	
	20th		2 Lieut. D.C. Platt N.O.R. to Hospital struck off strength.	
	21st		3 OR to Hospital struck off strength. 1 OR wounded to duty. 1 OR sent from Base & 2 OR from Hospital were taken on strength	

WAR DIARY
INTELLIGENCE SUMMARY
(Erase heading not required.)

Army Form C. 2118.

Place	Date	Hour	Summary of Events and Information	Remarks and references to Appendices
	21st July 16		Capt. W.C. L. MARQUE proceeded to U.K. on 14 days leave.	
	22nd		1 OR to Hospital struck off strength.	
	23rd		" " The Brigade was relieved by 22nd Bde. The Battalion sent 1st Royal Inniskillings & Divisional Reserve. The Battalion moved to la PIQUELLERIE went into Billets. "B" Teams rejoined.	
	24th		Day was spent in bathing, cleaning of equipment &c. (Lieut R.H. NAPIER proceeded to H.Q. ELNES for duty as Staff Lieut.	proceeded 22-7-16
			(Aar 3 (Clooijaus P.B.) (authority GHQ letter 3507 of 30.6.16.) was Struck off strength. } 34th 1 OR to Hospital struck off strength. 1 OR from Hospital taken on.	
	25th		1 OR to Hospital " " & 1 OR to Sick list struck off. 1 OR from " " confirmed as G.S.W. 1. One Sent to Hospitals (evacuated) taken on.	
	26th		1 OR from base taken on. 1 OR found now on death roll taken on.	J.F.E.
			1 OR sick. 1 OR to Hospital struck off strength.	

WAR DIARY
or
INTELLIGENCE SUMMARY.

Army Form C. 2118.

Place	Date	Hour	Summary of Events and Information	Remarks and references to Appendices
	29 July/18		IOR from Hospital taken on strength. IOR to Hospital struck off strength. Lieut Q.M.T MEDHURST proceeded to 3/7 K.R.Battalion 3rd Army was struck off strength (Authority AC/30/11 (0) d/23/7/18.) 2/Lieut Jn. MANN proceeds to 1 K.R.B. the Buffs (Authority GHQ 3rd Echelon 1364/5252.)	
	30		IOR from Hospital taken on strength and to Hospital struck off	
	31st		IOR to Hospital struck off strength.	Nil

C.H.Balston.
Lieut Col
Cmdg
(E. & W. KENT YEO) Bn. THE BUFFS

10th The Buffs
JULY/18

WAR DIARY
INTELLIGENCE SUMMARY

Monthly Summary
1st – 31st July 1918

Administrative. During the course of the month, 1 officer (2 Lieut J.W. MANN) + 3 Drafts of 11 O.R., 4 O.R., 40 O.R., joined the Battalion for duty. Their Bayonets on the whole was good, their average periods of service were 3½ years, 4¾ years, + 9½ years respectively. Lieut R.P. NAPIER left the Battalion for duty with H.Q., ETAPLES, as a Staff Lieut. Class 3 (Gazetted 7/8.)

The following courses were attended during the month:—

CANADIAN CORPS SCHOOL	—	AUBIN ST. VAAST. — General. — Lieut H. OXLEY.
" " "	—	" " 2 O.R.
" " "	—	" Lewis Gun 1 O.R.
1st ARMY INFTY. SCHOOL	—	HARDELOT — Infantry — 1 O.R.
" " "	—	VAUDRINGHEM — General — 2 Lieut C.F. BURT
" " "	—	" " 30 O.R.
" " "	—	" L. Gun 20 O.R.
" " "	—	" Bombing Lieut C.T.G. SWAINSON 1 O.R.

WAR DIARY
or
INTELLIGENCE SUMMARY.
(Erase heading not required.)

Army Form C. 2118.

Place	Date	Hour	Summary of Events and Information	Remarks and references to Appendices

1. Administration (contd)

1st Army Musketry Camp   Musketry   2 Lt W. CRAWR

       "   "   3 OR

       "   "   1 OR

1st Corps Gas School "NAMETZ"   Gas Course   2 Lieut. J.E. DODSON

HARDELOT   P. + B.T.   1 OR

           "   "   1 OR

2. Discipline. The Discipline of the Battalion continued excellent throughout the period.

3. Health. During the first week of the month there were a few cases of P.U.O. but since then no further cases have been reported, & the health of the Battalion has been good. No cases of infectious disease have been reported.

Army Form C. 2118.

WAR DIARY
or
INTELLIGENCE SUMMARY.
(Erase heading not required.)

Place	Date	Hour	Summary of Events and Information	Remarks and references to Appendices
			4. Ordnance Services Good	
			5. Supply " Good	
			6. Transport " Good	
			7. Operations & Training	
			On the 10th of month the Battalion moved from ENQUIN-	
			LES-MINES to HAM-EN-ARTOIS by motor lorries where it remained for	
			one night in Divisional Reserve. The following day the Battalion moved	
			into Brigade Reserve + marched to LA PIERRIÈRE + relieved the 2 C.R. Canadian	
			Regt.	
			Whilst in Brigade Reserve working parties were supplied by	
			the Battalion for work in the front line neighbourhood. During	
			the night of 16/17th 20 OR were killed + 9 OR wounded whilst on a	
			working party. Lt.Col. BUZZARD received a gun shot wound subsequently died of wounds	
			on the 28th of month. The Brigade was relieved by the 2 Gr. Brigade	

Operations & Training (contd.)
and went into Divisional Reserve. Battalion proceeded to
La MIQUELLERIE where training was commenced.

C P Bawton Lieut Col.
Comdg. (E. & W. KENT YEO) BN The BUFFS

Army Form C. 2118.

10 E Kent Rgt
SD 5

WAR DIARY
or
INTELLIGENCE SUMMARY.
(Erase heading not required.)

Instructions regarding War Diaries and Intelligence Summaries are contained in F. S. Regs., Part II. and the Staff Manual respectively. Title pages will be prepared in manuscript.

Place	Date	Hour	Summary of Events and Information	Remarks and references to Appendices
	1 Aug 1916		Battalion training at LA MIQUELLERIE. Battalion formed part of Brigade Support. MAJOR W.G. LITTLE removed from his makeshift sorrel by O.C. Finds Short of strength. TOR from Hospital taken on strength.	Refmap FRANCE 36A 1/100,000
	2 "		Battalion training at LA MIQUELLERIE. 10R to Hospital. Struck off strength. Battalion training at LA MIQUELLERIE. N.O.R. to Hospital. Struck off strength.	
	3.			
	4.		Battalion left LA MIQUELLERIE. Took over right sub section left sector (ST FLORIS) from 10th R.S.F. C.13 Company in the Keepers 7.D in Reserve, H.Q. in HINGETTE-LOCOSTRIQUE from 7.K Division.	
	5.		1 OR to Hospital. Struck off strength. 10R from 10K Division. Brigade notifies us that the Pension on our right have	

2353 Wt. W3544/1454 700,000 5/15 D.D.&L. A.D.S.S./Forms/C. 2118.

Place	Date	Hour	Summary of Events and Information	Remarks and references to Appendices
	5 Aug 16 (contd)		advanced their line, what the Battalion was to have prepared to move forward, should the trenches to our front be evacuated as they had been on our night to R bounded & 10R sick. Hospital truck offstrength. 10R from II Corps Bombing School. 10R from Base taken on strenth.	Ref Maps FRANCE 36 1/40.000
	6		The 22nd Brigade on night pushed forward their line but the Batt. was unable to do the same owing to considerable opposition. except on the right flank, where "B" Company pushed forward & book to keep in touch with 1st DEVONS on their right. 2 OR killed, 10R wounded & 3 OR sick to Hospital. Strength later on strength 910 off. strength. 10R from Hospital C. & A. Companies pushed forward to the line Q.2.a.5.0. to Q.2.C. Combat 5th Comparative little opposition in	

WAR DIARY
INTELLIGENCE SUMMARY

Army Form C. 2118.

Place	Date	Hour	Summary of Events and Information	Remarks and references to Appendices
	7 Aug 1918	(contd)	2 OR wounded, 1 OR sick to Hospital, Struck off Strength. "D" "A" Companies passed through "B" "C" Companies & pushed on to K.33 Central, but at 2pm "A" Coy. to Q.3. Central through LA HENNERIE to Q.3.d Central, but at 2pm "A" Coy. were counter-attacked on their right flank which drew back Co. to 16 join up with 229th Brigade who were stationed at Q.9.a.67 at 7pm. "D" "A" Companies pushed on to the W. Bank of the R. LYS again, but were unable to cross owing to all the Bridges being blown up. 4 OR to Hospital struck off Strength. The R.E. brought up 3 bridges which were utilised to cross the R. LYS at Q.3.d.77, Q.3.d.58, & Q.3.6.23, and dug in about 50 yards on East side. 29 OR found as a draft. Were taken on Strength. Casualties. 6 OR Killed, LT. R.H. ATKINSON, + 13 OR wounded, 1 OR (shell Gas)	Ref map FRANCE=36 1:40,000.
	9			
	10		Battalion patrolled actively to front which the enemy held with machine guns. Probably pushed out in front of their wire. 6 OR to Hospital struck off strength. 1 OR wounded (shell Gas)	

WAR DIARY
INTELLIGENCE SUMMARY.
(Erase heading not required.)

Army Form C. 2118.

Date	Hour	Summary of Events and Information	Remarks and references to Appendices
11 Aug 18		Battalion patrolled actively to front. 3 O.R. to Hospital chiefly off strength. Casualties. 1 O.R. killed, 4 O.R. wounded, 1 of whom subsequently died. 1 O.R. missing.	Ref map Ste Marie 36.A 1:40,000
12		At 9.30 pm "D" + "A" Companies endeavoured to push forward to late enemy works in K.34.a.21. & Q.4.c.6.8. The night was especially dark owing to the considerable strength of the enemy, and a counter-attack which was launched by him on our right flank, we were forced to withdraw back into the line previously occupied. "A" + "B" Companies relieved "D" + "A" in front line. 1 OR proceed to ETAPLES for disposal (authority G.H.Q. 2nd Ech. C.R. Nº 55au d/26.07/10 d/18.7.18) 1 OR to KOR. (authority G.H.Q. 2nd Ech. C.R. Nº 55au d/26.07/10 d/18.7.18) 1 OR to KOR. shuck off strength. Casualties 3 O.R. killed, 17 O.R. wounded (1 of whom subsequently died) 7 O.R. missing (2 of whom were wounded)	
13		Patrolled actively to front. LT. F.H. KEEK to Hospital + 17 OR to Hospital struck off strength 18 OR from Hospital 10 OR Reft.	
14		Hospital struck off strength 18 OR from hospital 10 OR Reft. taken over Chengh.	

WAR DIARY
INTELLIGENCE SUMMARY
(Erase heading not required.)

Army Form C. 2118.

Place	Date	Hour	Summary of Events and Information	Remarks and references to Appendices
	14 Aug 18		Battalion was relieved by 16th Sussex went into Battalion in support with 2 Companies from NYS CANAL K.31.d. to Q.1.a.80 & 2 Companies from Q.7.a.13 to Q.13.c.38.7.0& to hospital struck off strength 10R wounded. Notification received from 230 F. Ambulance that 18 OR previously admitted sick had been diagnosed wounded. Struck off strength. Battalion cleaned trenches & dug-outs. 10R to Hospital struck off strength. S.D.	
	15th			
	16th		Relieved at 10 p.m by 16th K.S.L.I. Brigade went into support C & A Companies in Reserve Line B & D Companies (taken over of OONET MALO, ST VENANT ROAD) in ANXOUS RES- HAVERSKERQUE Line & All Companies salvaged 10R wounded 5 OR from Hospital taken on strength 10R (Cooks Regt employed) struck off strength 2Lt W.E. ONIONS joined for duty taken on strength.	

WAR DIARY
or
INTELLIGENCE SUMMARY

Army Form C. 2118.

Place	Date	Hour	Summary of Events and Information	Remarks and references to Appendices
	17 Aug 15		Improved dug-outs & trenches. Lt. E.G. PORTER joined for duty. Wires taken on Strength. 3 O.R. from Hospital taken on Strength. 1 O.R. to Hospital Struck off Strength.	
	16 "		5 O.R. joining. 300 Sand-bags filled with ears of corn. 2 O.R. to Hospital Struck off Strength. 24 O.R. joined as draft. Wires taken on Strength.	
	17 "		8 O.R. harvested in neighbourhood of ROBECQ with a reaper. 150 men improved reserve trenches. 4 O.R. to Hospital Struck off Strength.	
	20 "		100 O.R. working on trenches. 60 wiring. 50 salvaging. 10 O.R. to Hospital Struck off Strength. 1 O.R. from Hospital & 1 O.R. joined as draft taken on Strength.	
	21 "		100 O.R. digging Reserve Line. 50 wiring. 50 salvaging. 3 O.R. to Hospital Struck of Strength. 1 O.R. from Hospital taken on Strength.	

WAR DIARY
or
INTELLIGENCE SUMMARY.
(Erase heading not required.)

Army Form C. 2118.

Place	Date	Hour	Summary of Events and Information	Remarks and references to Appendices
	22 Aug 1916		A Company remained in Reserve line. Remainder went into billets in ST FLORIS. 200 OR. used for wounding parties. 18 OR from Hospital taken on strength. 30 OR to Hospital struck off strength.	
	23 "d		50 OR wiring Remainder cleaned billets in ST FLORIS. which were in a very bad sanitary condition. Knusch knocked about by shell fire. 30 OR to Hospital struck off strength. two	
	24 "		75 OR wiring. 3 Companies cleaned billets in ST FLORIS Brigade was relieved & went into Divisional Reserve. Battalion being relieved by 10 K.S.L.I. went into billets in LA PIERRIERE 20 R. to Hospital struck off strength. 3 OR from Hospital taken on strength. 3 OR joined as a draft from 5th & 46 EAST YORK Batts. & 40 OR from 11th R.W. Surreys leave taken on strength.	
	25 "		Re-fitting line - organizing. 253 OR bathed at GUAS EQ Q ∞ 10R. 10 Hospital struck off strength.	

WAR DIARY
INTELLIGENCE SUMMARY

Place	Date	Hour	Summary of Events and Information	Remarks and references to Appendices
	Aug 16		Battalion relieved by 2/6 R.W.F. "B" Company marched to L'ESPESSES. went into billets. Remainder went into billets at COTTES	
	27th		2 Lt N. HOARE joined the Battalion for duty, was taken on the strength. 28 OR from Hospital + 108 as draft were taken on strength. Rifle has made inspection S.O.R. from Hospital taken on strength	
	28th		20R to Hospital struck off strength. Pre Order Buise PR Manuel 8.30 AM 10.10 AM	
	29th		"B" Company entrained at MILLERS at 10.41 pm back as unloading party to Brigade Group at HEILLY & Remainder entrained at MILLERS at 1.41 Am and arrived at HEILLY about 7.30 pm. Battalion went into dug-outs	Ref. maps Sheet 13d 1/40.000
	30th		in neighbourhood of J 13a. 4 OR proceeded to Bare for 6 months Tour of duty at home were struck off strength. 5 OR to Hospital struck off strength. 2nd Lt CAR Taylor + 2nd Lt C Boar and 5 OR from Base taken on strength	

WAR DIARY
or
INTELLIGENCE SUMMARY.

Army Form C. 2118.

Place	Date	Hour	Summary of Events and Information	Remarks and references to Appendices
	31st Aug 1916		The following Officers and 59 O.R. proceeded to Div'l Reception Camp. FRANVILLERS as 'B' teams. Major L.E. Bromley, 2/Lieut. J.H. Friend, 2/Lieut. T.A.S. ALLNARD, 2/Lieut. O.S. Hall, 2 wth. 2/Lt. H.E. Lawrance 2 wth. N.E. Daylen. The Battn. proceeded to MAUREPAS by motor lorries (B 15. central) area	HQ. Hdqrs. 2/C. NW Edilion 1/6

C.B.Balston
Lt. Col.
Commanding Kent Yeo. Battn. E. Kent Regt.

SUMMARY.
1st to 31st Aug 1918

1. <u>Administration</u>. During the month 3 drafts totalling 5 officers and 96 other ranks joined the Battalion. Their physique was good and their average period of service was 8 months.

   The following courses of instruction were attended.

Course	Place	Officer	other ranks
Cookery	CORCEQUE	—	1
Signalling	XI Corps School	—	2
Gas	"	2nd Lt W.E. Onions	1
General	"	" N.G. Wale	2
Lewis Guns	"	—	2
Bombing	"	—	1
Trench Mortar	"	—	1
Catering	CORCEQUE	—	1
Gas	XI Corps School	—	2
Coy Commanders		Capt. H.L. Alfrey	—

2. <u>Discipline</u>. The discipline of the Battalion continued excellent throughout the period.

3. <u>Health</u>. There have been 3 cases of suspected dysentery and a few cases of slight diarrhoea but the health of the Battalion may be called Good throughout the period.

4. <u>Ordnance Services</u>. Good.

5. <u>Supply Services</u>. Good.

6. <u>Transport Services</u>. Good.

7. <u>Operations & Training</u>.

   The Battalion after moving from LA MIQUELLERIE went into the line in the ST. FLORIS SECTOR. As the enemy began evacuating

7. Operations & Training Cont'd

evacuating his front trenches active operations immediately resulted by which we pushed forward our line about 200 yards; comparatively little opposition was met with and our casualties were light. In a further attempt on night 12/13th instant to take the enemy's works on the E of the RIVER LYS a complete reaction set in on the part of the enemy who opposed the advance with considerable vigour and launched a counter attack before we had reached our objective, we were accordingly compelled to withdraw to our original line on the LYS through LA HENNERIE and CALONNE.

When the Brigade was relieved and went into support the battalion put in a considerable amount of work both digging and wiring into the RESERVE Line and also harvested where the reapers could not travel by plucking the ears of corn and filling some 200 sand bags per diem. The battalion also during this time had eight men working as reapers from 8 a.m. to 8 p.m. daily and 3 men stacking corn. On relief the battalion moved to LA PIERRIERE and then to COTTES and entrained at LILLIERS on 29th instant for the SOMME front.

C.H. Balston
Lt Col.
Commanding KENT YEO Battalion E. KENT REGT.

WAR DIARY or INTELLIGENCE SUMMARY

Army Form C. 2118.

Place	Date	Hour	Summary of Events and Information	Remarks and references to Appendices
		8 AM	Remained at B.21.a.	
			20 OR from hospital taken in 3rd Bugh. 16 OR to hospital struck off strength	
	2		Rabalia moved up preparatory of assembly 5.20 am L.B.30.b at 8.45 am moved to C.27.a. "C" Company took over portion of front line from C.22.a. 04. to C.27.b.9.9. Battalion heavily shelled all day with H.E. & gas. 2 OR killed Capt E.P. Delaney R.A.M.C. & 12 OR wounded, 6 OR wounded (shell gas) 4 OR to F.A. struck off strength.	
	3		"C" & "D" Companies moved to the C.18.C.7.4.1 C.22.C.4.0. "A" & "B" Companies in support in DELVA TRENCH. Batt. H.Q. and "D" Coy in Reserve at C.27.a. 6.8.	
		2 PM	Lieut S.E. Ommen to medical shell gas. Captain L.C. Kernighan wounded & sent to England - struck off strength. 12 OR to hospital struck off strength	
	4		"C" & "D" Companies took over line from the 229 Brigade from C.22.a.y.n. - C.24.C.7.0. "A" Coy in support on C.22.C "D" Coy in DELVA TRENCH C.21.E. Objective [?] point reported MIDINETTE TRENCH respected	
			14 OR to Hospital struck off strength	

Place	Date	Hour	Summary of Events and Information	Remarks and references to Appendices
	Sept 5th		Ref Map 62C N.E. 1/20,000 Battalion took over the 23rd Brigade frontage from C24 a.0.4 to C30 c.0.4. Captured MIDINETTE trench at 1.15 p.m. Pushed on at 8 p.m. and took west from D20 & 21. In a further attempt to advance, owing to M.G. opposition we had to withdraw to D20 & 21 trench again. Lieut C.S. Bowley wounded to Hosp. 4 OR wounded to Hosp. 4 OR sick to F.A. struck off strength.	
	6		Started the attack again at 8 a.m. with "D" & "A" Companies in front line, "C" in support, and "B" in reserve. We reached the final objective at 3.45 p.m. and took up an outpost line in E20 & E26a. A defensive flank was formed in E19d, as the 4th Division had not got as far forward as ourselves. 3 OR killed in action. 12 OR wounded to Hosp. Struck off strength. 2" Lieut C.S. Smith sick to F.A. 6 OR sick to F.A. struck off strength 1 OR from Hosp. on 10/5/16 the 10th K.S.L.I. had passed through the Battalion concentrated in E20 & E26a. Battalion H.Q. E19d 1.3	C.R.
	7		2 OR wounded to Hosp. struck off strength. 3 OR sick to Hosp. struck off strength.	C.R.
	8		Remained same place. 3 OR sick to F.A. struck off strength. 1 OR from Hosp. taken on strength.	C.R.

WAR DIARY or INTELLIGENCE SUMMARY

Army Form C. 2118.

Place	Date	Hour	Summary of Events and Information	Remarks and references to Appendices
	Sept 9		Salvaged from TEMPLEUX trench to NURLU - PERONNE road. Revd. of J.G. Everison 2Lt. to F.A. 1 OR from Hosp. taken on strength.	
	10		Took over the front line from the 14th R.H. from F13b 6.0 to F19d 1.5 incl. "B" & "C" Coys + half "D" Coy in line; remainder of "D" Coy in bivouac at F19a 1.6. "A" Coy + Battalion H.Q. at E23d 2.6. 1 OR killed in action. 1 OR drift from England taken on strength. 3 OR from Hosp. taken on strength. Point kueles front line very weak throughout. Sniping very severe.	
	11		Consid'ble M.G. + artillery fire during day. 1 OR died of wounds. 11 OR wounded to Hosp. 2 OR from Base taken on strength.	
	12		"A" Coy relieved "B" Coy + 2 platoons of "D" Coy. Relieved 2 platoons of "C" Coy. Latter went into Ouyeport + "B" Coy into Reserve. 3 OR wounded to Hosp. 1 OR Rich to F.A. 3 n'gte off strength. 2 OR from Hosp taken on strength. 2nd Lt RE Jackson Newport Reid Lus to Hosp. Several Enemy artillery fire	
	13		1 OR killed in action. Lieut J.S. Matthews wounded to Hosp. 1 OR wounded to Hosp.	
	14		Relieved by 24th W.R. + moved to K2 h.v.d. Began to hopel. 1 OR wounded to Hosp	

WAR DIARY or INTELLIGENCE SUMMARY

Army Form C. 2118.

Place	Date	Hour	Summary of Events and Information	Remarks and references to Appendices
	Sept 15		Refilling. 2 OR from Hosp. taken on strength.	
	16		Moved to area between FAUSTINE QUARRY & K5 f Central. 1 OR from Hosp. taken on strength. 2 OR to Hosp. Struck off strength.	
	17		"A" Coys. held over the front line from the 15th SUFFOLKS on Z 1 C. "B" 8 OR wounded to Hosp. 4 OR S.I.d. to F.A. struck off strength, 10 OR from Hosp. taken on strength. 5 OR Trans. to Draft. Struck off strength. 50 "C" & "D" Coys. moved at 3-30 a.m. Battn H.Q. to GEORGES COPSE. "C" & "D" Coys to trenches vacated by "A" & "B" Coys. While the latter moved into SUNKEN ROAD L1b. our orders were to pass through the 15th SUFFOLKS	
	18		who took the 16th SUSSEX Amer to attg. the GREEN LINE CONNOR POST and SUNKEN ROAD L5.d.f.d. in F28d, L1b.j L1b. the barrage started at 8-30 a.m. and followed by this. A & B Companies advanced to the RED LINE. A 25.d. 3.0 to F30c. 9.1. CARBINE, ZOGDA Trenches in readiness in the enemy who took up a position, F30c.1.9 to F30c.3.6. bring to our own barrage coming down on us. Capt. N.L.Guffrey & 2nd Lieut E.G.Porter OHS killed in action. 16 OR killed in action. 7 OR died of wounds. 48 OR wounded to Hosp. 2 OR missing. 4 OR sick to F.A. struck off strength. 5 OR from Hosp. taken on strength.	

WAR DIARY or INTELLIGENCE SUMMARY

Army Form C. 2118.

Place	Date	Hour	Summary of Events and Information	Remarks and references to Appendices
	Sep. 19		Considerable artillery activity. "C" & "D" Coys relieved "A" & "B" Coys in the front line. Took up a position in 200dA + CARIBINE Trenches F30c with posts in SUNKEN ROAD F30c b&k F30a o3 + CARIBINE Trench F30c. 6 OR from Hosp. taken on strength. 6 OR struck off strength.	
	20		The front traversed. 1 OR wounded to Hosp. 5 OR rejoined from Hosp. taken on strength. 2 OR from Hosp. taken on strength.	
	21		At 5-40 a.m. B. & C. Coys in the front line and "A" Coy in support formed up on road running N.W. + S.E. in F30c + advanced under a barrage to later the BLUE LINE from A20c.52 to A20c.48. The hour W. of Z00 Trench was reached, and one of the two hills penetrated but a tremendous M.G. fire was met here + no further advance could be made. A withdrawal was necessitated by the flag stations on the left coming back. The front line of a few men of "A" Coy, the Battalion was relieved in the evening by the 1st SUFFOLKS, & took up a position in SHERWOOD Trench in the neighbourhood of F28 c 5.0.	
1 Hosp 62.8.NW ½ 20.000			Capt. C.E. Hatfield + 2nd Lieut H.C. Colley + 12 OR killed in action. Lieut C.B. Turgeming + 2nd Lieut W.S. Hoare wounded to Hosp. 38 OR wounded to Hosp. 1 OR died of wounds. Lieut F.D. Wilkinson wounded remaining. 6 OR wounded remaining. 20 OR missing. 8 OR from Hosp. taken on strength. 5 OR rejoined F.A. struck off strength.	

WAR DIARY or INTELLIGENCE SUMMARY

Army Form C. 2118.

Place	Date	Hour	Summary of Events and Information	Remarks and references to Appendices
Sept	22		Took over GREEN LINE from CONNOR POST to L.H. Quebec. 3 O.R. sick to F.A. struck off strength.	
	23		Front French GREEN LINE relieved by 8th LONDONS. Battalion was distributed in depth in BOLSOVER SWITCH & SHERWOOD TRENCH ready to reinforce them. 3 O.R. killed in action, 1 O.R. died of wounds, 3 O.R. wounded to Hosp.	C.O. C.O.
	24		Battalion moved to D.30.C. Evacuated for the night. 1 O.R. wounded to hospital.	C.O.
	25		Entrained at PERONNE & proceeded to VILLERS-BRETONNEUX, marched to AUBIGNY & billeted there.	C.O.
	26		Remained in billets at AUBIGNY.	
	27		Entrained at HEILLY at about 8 p.m.	
	28		Detrained at LILLERS about 9.30 a.m. marched to rail billets at ALLOUAGNE. The following officers joined the Battalion for duty from England & were later on the strength: Lieut. D.S. Shaver, Lieut. F.W.I. Smithers, 2.Lieut. R.S. Charge, 2 Lieut. F.R. Morley, 2 Lieut. H.B. Walls, 2 Lieut. H.B. Watts, 2 Lieut. E.R. Church, 2 Lieut. W.A. Powell.	C.O.
	29		At ALLOUAGNE refitting & organising. The following officers joined W. Baker to duty from England & were taken on the strength: 2 Lieut. S.W.P. Pamphlen, 2 Lieut. L.F. Smith, 2 Lieut. J. Kitley, 2 Lieut. H.G. Thompson, 2 O.R. to Hosp, struck off strength. 2 O.R. from Hosp taken on strength.	C.O.

WAR DIARY
or
INTELLIGENCE SUMMARY.

Place	Date	Hour	Summary of Events and Information	Remarks and references to Appendices
	Sept. 30		at ALLOUAGNE refitting & reorganising. 43 OR joined as a draft from England & were taken on the strength. C.H.Batten Lt. Col. Comdg. 10th East Yorks Regt. C in P	
			SUMMARY of OPERATIONS.	
			The month of September 1918 proved to be the hardest experienced by the battalion since it was formed. With an interval from the 14th to the 19th, the Battalion was in action continuous active service conditions were experienced from the 2nd to the 24th. Starting along the CANAL DU NORD between MOISLAINS & HAUT ALLAINES, the battalion was in the line, or the forefront of the battle most of the way till RIFLE PIT TRENCH & ZOGDA TRENCH N.E. of HARGICOURT were reached, and in the further advance N.E. of this. The enemy defence till this had been very severe, for instance, for machine guns admirably placed at PIMPLE POST, F28c, had not fewer 200 rounds & only one of the 5 guns were withdrawn, our barrage however in this sector along the RONSSOY - HARGICOURT Road had done admirable work.	
			In a further attempt to advance from ZOGDA TRENCH, F30c, to QUENNEMONT FARM in N.21.d. severe opposition was met with from M.Gs. our artillery also failing hard, and the remnant of the battalion were compelled to withdraw to their original starting line ZOGDA TRENCH. At the end of the month the battalion were taken out of the line and entrained to KILLERS, marching from there and billets at AUBIGNY.	
			C.H.Batten Lt. Col.	

Army Form C. 2118.

WAR DIARY
or
INTELLIGENCE SUMMARY.
(Erase heading not required.)

Instructions regarding War Diaries and Intelligence Summaries are contained in F. S. Regs., Part II. and the Staff Manual respectively. Title pages will be prepared in manuscript.

Place	Date	Hour	Summary of Events and Information	Remarks and references to Appendices
	Feb 14th 1916		**Administrative.**	
	30th		During the month the strength of the Battalion averaged 10 Officers and 2nd Lay 27 Officers & 97 [?] in ranks and 12 months.	
			Discipline. The discipline of the Battalion continued excellent throughout the period.	
			Health. The health of the Battalion during the past month has been good. No cases of infectious disease have been notified.	
			Ordnance Service — good.	
			Supply Service — good.	
			Transport Service — good.	

C H Ralston
Lieut. Col.
Comdg. East Kent Regt "The Buffs"

10th Buff/s
10th The Buffs
Army Form C. 2118.
Oct 18

WAR DIARY
or
INTELLIGENCE SUMMARY.
(Erase heading not required.)

VOL.
PAGE 1.

Month: OCT 1918.

Place	Date	Hour	Summary of Events and Information	Remarks and references to Appendices
FRANCE 36 S.W. 1/20,000	October 1		Relieved 9th R.W.F. 19th Divn RICHEBOURG Section. "A"+"B" in front line. R.H.A.T.W.S.N. Battn Hqrs Rue du Bois. Coy HQrs T11 & T13 fd. Lieut R.H. ATKINSON sent to hospital. O.C. Major F.E. BEAVAN 25th R.W.F. was evacuated to hospital sick off strength	See Reg't hist 36 1/40,000
	2		Battalion relieved by Batt HQRS (R.H.Q.) Hospital Farm W.9 KILLIES T11 & T13 fd. no enemy seen. Lieut R.H. ATKINSON from Hospital rejoined & offs&mens C/B. 3 O.R. from H.P.M. "A" Bn to W.O. taken on strength. 1 O.R. Field wounded on strength.	
	3		Advanced at Dawn to LA BASSÉE - AUBERS - FROMELLES line & on to head T16 b+c on to Sugar Factory (T15 c.16) Thence through GRANDE RUE - STANCHIN & +13 Coys, dug in on line V.14 + rd. B. coys, V13 a + d. C. coy U.136. 3 O.R. injured at Hood officer off strength & O.R. sick & F.A. struck off strength.	
	4		SUFFOLKS moved through us at 0800 and took final objective WAVRIN-LATTRE without being held up. O.35 d.c. but advanced in support by SUFFOLKS could not get on to 2nd objective as 55th Divn on right was held up by M.G.'s on S. side of Canal. E. Bn rest in front line to held gap between 1st SUFFOLKS and 55th Divn. 2 O.R. wounded to hospital struck off strength. 1 O.R. sick & F.A. struck off strength.	

WAR DIARY / INTELLIGENCE SUMMARY

Army Form C. 2118.

VOL.
PAGE 2.

Place	Date	Hour	Summary of Events and Information	Remarks and references to Appendices
Ref. Map FRANCE 36 S.W. 1/20,000	October 5		Enemy Stationary. Fairly heavy shelling. 35th Divn on right advanced being slightly left. Bn also held up. C. Coy withdrawn behind D. line taken by us N and S between U.8 c and q and U.14 and 15 as far S as V.15c.3.3. Bn HQ V.14.6.0. 1 O.R. killed & F.A. struck off strength.	
	6		Enemy Stationary. Situation fairly quiet. Support line (our) ordered to be line of protection. Digging commenced to strengthen. Enemy trenches must be reached by reserve Battn to form protection line. 1 O.R. struck off strength.	
	7		Relieved the SUFFOLKS on front line from U.5.b. central to U.6.d. central. A Coy on left, then C.B. and B. to southward. Battn forward HQ moved to U.6.d.4.4. Many patrols by day & night were sent out the next 3 days to ascertain position of enemy posts, and to keep back in cover to whatever posts they occupied. to make a strong defensive Line. 10 ORs wounded 5th Batt Rfle, 53 DOW on right. 3 ORs killed in action. 2 OR wounded & to hosp. 2 OR R.R.U. F.A. struck off strength. 1 OR wounded shell gas. 1 OR struck off strength.	
	8		Forward Battn H.Q. moved to U.11.a.8.3. Fairly heavy shelling in front line from enemy M.G's and snipers very active. 2nd Lieut R.C.J. KETTLE, 2nd Lieut P.C. TULLY, 2nd Lieut R.H. WRIGHT, 2nd Lieut H.J. WENBAN, 2nd Lieut C.F. PACKMAN, joined for duty. 2nd Lieut J.N. ASHCROFT, and 2nd Lieut ——— from Base taken on strength. 3 ORs 2nd Lieut F.W. MORLEY died of wounds taken on strength. 5 OR to hospital. 2 OR struck off strength 2 OR struck to F.A. wounded. 15 to hospital. 1 OR wounded. 2 OR struck off strength.	

WAR DIARY or INTELLIGENCE SUMMARY

Army Form C. 2118.
VOL. **PAGE 3**

Place	Date	Hour	Summary of Events and Information	Remarks and references to Appendices
FRANCE 36.S.W 20.000				
	9		Relief by the 6th Div. Rd Division relieved by 1/1 at 0600-0730. Company and Bn parties of K.S.L.I. when had assembled in Roney Wood rejoined 24 men B.Coy. started at 4 am and reached Ors. General gas casualties 5 OR wounded to Hospl struck off strength. 14 OR admitted to Hospl. General struck off strength. 1 OR from Hospl Taken on strength.	
	10		On arrival at Ors section of MGs from Bde. Coy. were billeted by us in billets. At 10.00 returned to Roger Ron Rejoined Bn. 1/5 Duty RFA and 6th Bn Recrmen had a friendly 010. 1 OR Killed in action 9 OR wounded to Hospl struck off strength. 2/Lt T.E. DODSON killed in action. 1 OR to Hospl struck off strength.	
	11		On arrival at Ors. change of billets. OR's returned to use with Coy masters. Units guided as ordered at 4am-0715 & 0720 Bn Back the uper line again. 090 conduit through 0820-0915-0821 U 2 c 50 by C.O. & 2 Lts Poster Coy Kirk. Reconnaissance made for 14.30 by C.O.T. & 2 Lts Poston Coys. 1 OR wounded to Hospl struck off strength.	
	12		C.O reconnoitre Bridge in morning over river Pinker. Bn. Baths. Chipping of Cpl., Pl. Sgts & Lt. Pn. 2nd Lieut E.S. WILLIAMS, 2nd Lieut F.MOYSEY and 2/Lt R.M. R.H. HARDIMAN joined for duty and joined Bn. 6 OR from Hospl Taken on strength. 2 OR 1 Hospl struck off strength.	
	13		Bn went to Baths. Bn returned to OFFICERS in original how of village by Coys. Capt. Le Duty with A Coy. Lt. CAMPBELL D.Coy. 2/Lt from SUFFOLK's report to Coys. 1 OR announced to Hospl struck off strength. 2/Lt E. REED Hospl taken on strength. 3 OR from Hospl taken on strength.	

WAR DIARY or INTELLIGENCE SUMMARY

Army Form C. 2118.

VOL.
PAGE 4

Month and Year: **OCT 1918**

Place	Date	Hour	Summary of Events and Information	Remarks and references to Appendices
FRANCE 36 S.W. 1/20,000	14		2nd Lieut LINN with minor approach along railway at U.5.b. & when 0.35.b. returned O.R. to H.Q.M. should oft strength.	One
	15		Enemy endeavouring to make 12 objective from V.14.c.0 RÉSOIR SANTES, when completed Batts. occupy present front line. The SUSSEX the right line of Resistance reconnaissance carried out. Batt. occupied old front line. Established Batt. H.Q. also R.A.P. at QUINQUIEUS. B.Coy moved to S.E. Corner of U.6.d. to form defensive flank. remainder SUFFOLKS took 164 B.M. to be on of SUFFOLKS moving forward. B Coy to protect it's left to the East. En. but respected at 1500 right boy on Each thought V.16.44 digging covers from M.Gs. & T.M. also to work with Right Centre in Via Left besides fought in between P.5.b. left Coy to handle P.31.a. Pat. at pushing through RÉSOIR. Batt. support établie U.6.9. 2 Lieut J.E.B. BARNETT killed he duly taken on strength to on from HQ shortly on strength.	One
	16		2nd Lieut T.E. DODSON's body found and buried at O.34.d.9.1.B. 8cms. B.4444,6 R.Q.M. Sgt. Butter Left of 53rd Div. Ength of SUFFOLKS. 4.0.34 Q.M. Wound & support of Strength. I on strength. I hour church of strength.	One
	17		Batt. reinforcing front line relieved by SUFFOLKS at 12.10 Coys were moving forward to EMMERIN line Batt.s Batt. H.Q at P.32.E.3 also B Coy at P.14 to Batt. ordered beyond the 11 SUFFOLKS & have held on railway line to MENCHIN (very doubtful) with 11 SUFFOLKS & whole line in Regulation to by presented with 15 & 2nd went.	One

WAR DIARY of INTELLIGENCE SUMMARY

Army Form C. 2118.

VOL.
PAGE. 5
OCT. 1918.

Place	Date	Hour	Summary of Events and Information	Remarks and references to Appendices
FRANCE 36 S.E. 1/40000	October 17 (contd)		In line as before. B. Coy in D in left. No objection - Road East of FACHES was reached approx 18.30 no opposition - patrols were established slightly east of said road. No sign of enemy but railway bridge of W? found just at crossroads at FACHES blown up. Buffs relieved by 2/5" WELSH of 2ST. 18.30 at 21.30. 230" Bob in reserve. Buffs in 2 ranks 1 W.O. at WATTIGNIES V.G. at W1 d.9.9. No known Pioneer standard bridge. 6 Offrs. R.E. signal. 2 O.R. from Coast Coy at WATTIGNIES. Fort 6 Head struck off strength. 2 O.R. from Head. taken on strength. 40 R to 230. L.T.M.B. struck off strength	
	18		Battalion marched to billets at LESQUIN field centre a 13.05. Coys in HQR R01 15 H.Q.0 struck off strength. 401 from troops taken on strength.	
	19		Battalion marched to billets in GP SAINGHIN R34 P39 at mg arrived 16.30. HQ in 63. Reference Lille toy Carnonfagére	
Belgium 34 S.W. 30000	20		Battalion moved to billets at BRISIEUX. HQ in NIGC 3.3. No stragglers. 4 O.R. to Head. struck off strength	
	21		At BRISIEUX. Les Loos and air bathing alongmy Batt at HQ. The morning improved by some men to SUFFOLKS permission to bath. The buffs asked fell in their lines as he made up places wished to get to for which their Lt Coln informing. 2 O.R. to Head. struck off strength.	

WAR DIARY
INTELLIGENCE SUMMARY.

Army Form C. 2118.

VOL.
PAGE 6

Place: Belgium 3/S.W. B:000

Date	Hour	Summary of Events and Information	Remarks and references to Appendices
October 22		Battalion in training. Concert given by the Buffs at 18:30. 2 O.R. to Hosp. struck off strength.	
23		C.O. Confirms Regular I.O. wounded 14" R.H. on first line of transport from O15c 5.0 to Chau de la Marken. Horses due S. to O27c 1.0. no C.O. or 2nd in command. Relief cancelled. Battn. to stand fast. 1400 C.O. Conference re training programme. 2nd Lieut. E.W. CHURCH, 2/Lt. F.J. SMITH & 2nd Lieut. E. MOYSEY, admitted to Hosp. struck off strength. 2 O.R. to Hosp. struck off strength. 1 Hosp. struck off strength.	
24		Bn. 14" R.H. in line. Bn. H.Q. at MARQUAIN. B" Coy reported no at BAISIEUX. Enemy shelled billets. 1 O.R. wounded to Hosp. struck off strength. 1 O.R. sick to Hosp. struck off strength.	
25	20:30	Battalion at ORCQ evacuated — assembled at LAMAIN. AIRODION & Regt Patrols out to location M.G. position of heavy M.G. fire reported from B.H.Q. area at O26c 75.35. Support Coy "B" H.Q. O26b.05.60. "C" Coy A left of line from O15c.8.6 – O15a.26. C Coy centre O21a.45 – O15 O6.85. A Coy right of line O21e.11 – O26 a.16.55. Patrols out during night. Had touch with enemy south & south-eastwards of L". 17's heavily bombed & shelled. 2/Lt. W.A. COUNSELL & 5 O.R. wounded to Hosp. struck off strength. 5 O.R. to Hosp. struck off strength.	

WAR DIARY or INTELLIGENCE SUMMARY

Army Form C. 2118. VOL. PAGE. 7.

Place	Date	Hour	Summary of Events and Information	Remarks and references to Appendices
BELGIUM 37 S.W. 1/20,000	26		Remained at OREQ. Nothing of importance happened. Enemy still offering resistance with M.Gs. Very active. 1 O.R. wounded to Hosp. struck off strength. 1 O.R. from Hosp. taken on strength. 1 O.R. killed in action. 1 O.R. wounded to Hosp. struck off strength. 3 O.Rs. joined as 1st reinforcements in Field.	
	27		At OREQ. Went patrols out to keep touch with enemy. 0330 Bn. relieved from Hosp. taken on strength. 2 O.Rs. sent to F.A. struck off strength. 6 O.R. from Hosp. taken on strength.	
	28		Relieved on the Line by the 16 SUSSEX and 15 SUFFOLKS to organise Reserve. Marched out 2115. left O.Rs proceeded out Brigade Reserve at MARQUAIN. 2 O.R. to Hosp. struck off strength.	
	29		At MARQUAIN. Bn arrived 0130. Staying Resting. Yet Bn. had on Reserve. 3 O.R. to Hosp. struck off strength. 1 O.R. wounded struck off.	
	30		At MARQUAIN. Training refitting recreation. Relieved by 25 R.W.F. and 4 No's marched & billets in HERTAIN. Lieut. T.P.S. AYLWARD M.C. wounded Shell gun to Hosp struck off strength. 3 O.R. wounded shell gun to Hosp struck off strength.	

WAR DIARY

Army Form C. 2118.

VOL.
PAGE 8

INTELLIGENCE SUMMARY.

(Erase heading not required.)

Place	Date	Hour	Summary of Events and Information	Remarks and references to Appendices
Belgium	30th Sept		at HERTAIN training, refitting & reorganising. Capt. G.W. BISSETT & 2nd Lieut. R.T. STRANGE + 1 O.R. to Hospital, Attack off Strength, 12 O.R. from Base taken on strength.	
			B. Brown Major	
October 1-31	31		SUMMARY of OPERATIONS. The Battalion since leaving ALLOUAGNE has been moving forward steadily keeping in touch with the rapid retirement of the enemy. The operations during the month have not been severe, and any resistance the enemy showed was short lived. With the exception of a spell near BASSE RUE when crossing to the BLYS on our right being held up, we were unable for a short time to continue our advance. The operation all through the month has taken the form of machine gun nests. Casualties were light throughout. Two officers were killed towards the end of the month when the enemy began to slow down his retirement eventually coming to a standstill in front of TOURNAI and useful patrol work was carried out and much information gleaned respecting enemy defences, and two me[n] Canal of the Escaut was left by the enemy to hinder our advance. Were mined roads, railway bridges blown up, & further delay was made within a few hundred yards of our front line. Several M.G.s which were set in action both by day & night. On the 29th the Battalion was relieved in the tretching [trenching] South of SUFFOLKS & the 16th SUSSEX & went into Brigade Reserve on the 30th. The time by the 15th 231st Brigade was Divisional Reserve & reorganisation in the Brigade area. Relieved by the 231st Brigade, who relieved us proceeded units carried on & reorganisation commenced in the form of football, refitting & reorganising etc. O/carried.	

WAR DIARY
or
INTELLIGENCE SUMMARY

Army Form C. 2118.

VOL.
PAGE 9.

OCT 1918

Place	Date	Hour	Summary of Events and Information	Remarks and references to Appendices

October 1st to 31st. **ADMINISTRATIVE**

1. During the month no draft totalling 9 officers and 5 O.R. joined the Battalion. Their hygeen was good and their average period of service was twelve months.

The following courses of instruction were attended:-

Courses	Place	Officers	O. Ranks
Gas	XI Corps School MARETZ	{2nd D.S. MARCUS} {2nd J.S. GILLETT}	2
Cookery	Vickery School LILLERS		
Gas	XI Corps School		2
Lewis Gun	III Corps CAMICHES		1
Signals	Marching Signal School CHOCQUES		8
S.O.'S.	III Corps BREVRES	2nd H.S. DURSTON	3
Lewis Gun	G.H.Q. School	2nd C.W. HICKSON	
Light Course	Army School of Light	Capt J.T.H. FRIEND	

2. **Discipline.** The discipline of the Battalion has been good throughout the period

3. **Health.** There have been no cases of infectious diseases. The health of the Battalion may be called good throughout the period.

4. **Ordnance Services.** Good

5. **Supply Services.** Good

6. **Transport Services.** Good, 3 Riding horses urgently needed.

J.S. Brown
Major
-Comg 10th (E.v. W. Kent XOO) Bn the Buffs
(East Kent Regt)

WAR DIARY
or
INTELLIGENCE SUMMARY.

(Erase heading not required.)

Army Form C. 2118.

Sheet 230/74
Vol
10 E Ment R 'B'

Place	Date	Hour	Summary of Events and Information	Remarks and references to Appendices
HERTAIN	1 Nov		At HERTAIN Battalion parade training for entry into Tournai. CO & officers reconnoitred main line of resistance of specialists reconnoitred in afternoon. COS conference at 17.30. Duty party went to main road of resistance. Weed not for as during night & started from on strength.	Sheet 37 BELGIUM 1/40,000
			CAPT G.W. BISSETT/RAMC attached to Hospital 2nd R.T. EVANS RE to Hospital Sick Leave Church of strength	WJW
	2		At HERTAIN Battalion carried out transport for COs inspection at O.R.S. Bath Parade Dining Party. GOC conference 17.30. 30 O.Rs to Hospital Check of strength 2/Lt W.H. KURER 17th MC & sick as No 10	WJW
	3		At HERTAIN Cleaning, preparing for RCCs inspection 10th O.Rs to Hospital from hospital to the own ding.	WJW
	4		1000 Inspection of Battalion by R.S.C Commander of 21 M 6 brigade General F. (Richardson) 1/20783. Lt Col MATHER, DS MATHER, A (length down) Lt Col Bell very pleased with the Battalion turn out. Afternoon remainder inspected and a cross country run 10 officers MARQUAIN In afternoon by compagnies. The CO gave 7 O.R's to hospital is Suggesting as usual in evening.	WJW

P 419

WAR DIARY or INTELLIGENCE SUMMARY

Army Form C. 2118.

Sheet 2 Vol

Place	Date	Hour	Summary of Events and Information	Remarks and references to Appendices
HERTAIN	1400	5th	At HERTAIN. Training & re-fitting. Battalion paraded at 0830. 50 ranks from hospital taken on strength. To ranks to hospital, struck off.	M/W
		6th	At HERTAIN. Training & re-fitting. Battalion paraded at 0830.	M/W
			10 ranks to hospital struck off strength. 30 cross country run from pen boy.	
		7th	At HERTAIN. Training & re-fitting. Battalion paraded at 0830. COs conference of Platoon Officers & ranks at 1130. COs conference at 1130. 20 ranks & hospital struck off church. Major EF Pemberton DSO struck off strength being on senior officers course at ALDERSHOT. 10 ranks from hospital taken on strength.	M/W
			Wire received from Brigade that enemy believed withdrawn & 800 Battalion stood ready to move onward. 0830 Information received that enemy had withdrawn. Battalion moved at 1115 and arrived at TOURBOURG - DE LILLE at 14.45. Battalion HQ 0.29.6.0.6. Enemy shelled outskirts AV. XXXX Casualties 2 killed 2 wounded. "B" Coy took over duties of enemy picket 6 Coy. Duke of Boulevard Company kill. Co's Western outskirts of TOURNAI, holding Boulevard DE LEOPOLD on left A on right. Enemy holding EASTERN BANK of SCHELDT. Our kind of TOURNAI the Boulevard (Western outskirts of TOURNAI). Enemy & little	M/W
		9th	During night Sgt Russell patrol went out to TOURNAI & found he enemy had evacuated ridge. Escorted W/ patrol & enemy in occupation.	

WAR DIARY
or
INTELLIGENCE SUMMARY.

(Erase heading not required.)

Army Form C. 2118.

Sheet 3.
Vol. —

Place	Date	Hour	Summary of Events and Information	Remarks and references to Appendices
TOURNAI	Oct 8th 1918		At 7TH All Russian series SCHELDT blown up. We took possession of the town. S.O.Rarts from Hospital taken on Church.	BELGIUM Sheet 37 1/40.000 A/W
		10ᴬ	At F. d. LILLE. Evacuating wounded took "Bleams" lines. The Battalion King "Queen" of Belgium visited TOURNAI in evening. S.O.Rarts from Hospital taken on Church. S.O.Rarts to Hospital church off	A/W
			At F. d. LILLE. 9h 0930. Brigade announced KOS.— Hostilities crease at 11.00. More cancelled no time. At 11.00 orders known rest was confirmed. 11.15 Battalion members through TOURNAI proceeding East. Arrived at MONTREUIL-AU-BOIS at 17:30 Billets for night. 1.0 Bank to Hospital church off church	A/W
			10.00 am MONTREUL AU BOIS Ana church C.N.E. attending in memory of ESCANETTE 13.00. Bat Hq. 8.3a 74 on Route	A/W
	2ᴷ		At ESCANETTE. Battalion clearing roads + having 16:30 CoS Conference. Blood received orders + cross bridge WEST. 2 O.R. to Hospital church off church.	BELGIUM SHEET 28 1/W 1.40000 Sheet 37 1/40000 A/W
	4ᴷ		10.00 of ESCANETTE and marched to HERLIEGIES arriving 12.30. Batt Hq. R2C.44. 2LTS CJ FORT + F L HARRIS joined the Battalion F.D. 2 O.R. from hospital crosse taken on Church	A/W

WAR DIARY
INTELLIGENCE SUMMARY.
(Erase heading not required.)

Army Form C. 2118.

Sheet 4
Vol

Place	Date	Hour	Summary of Events and Information	Remarks and references to Appendices
HERQUEGIES	5	0700	At HERQUEGIES. 0645. A/C Coy Commenced Repair of No.1 formed working party for repairing roads, filling in mine craters etc. They were relieved at 1100 by remainder of A/C & B Coy.	A/W
	6		R.H.Q. Coys formed working party. Coys relieved at A/C Coy. at 1100	A/W
	7		A/C Coy formed working party as above. Relieved by B/C Coy at 1100	A/W
			At 1600 received orders of a move to BARRY and HAUT TRIEU. S.O.S. Gas Alarm Apparatus Taken down though	
	15		At 0930 Batt. marched to BARRY & HAUT TRIEU arriving there at 1200. Batt Hd.Qrs W.10.57. 10 Ranks to Hospital. Quiet Night.	BELGIUM (Sheet 3?) 1/40.000
BARRY			At BARRY 0915 A/C Coys. Hd.Qrs formed working parties on roads 703A.N.W/railway from Q.35.d.8.2. Working in a central point	A/W
			Quiet day. Clearing away obstructions etc. Relieved at 12.15 by A/C Coys. Operation Training and Musketry & a Class for Young NCOs formed	A/W
	20		O/K. A/C Coys. Hd.Qrs of R.Q. formed working party as on previous day. Were relieved at 12.15 by B Coy. Lt. G.F. TODD found for duty eg Ranks to Hospital. Although 5 Tanks	A/W

WAR DIARY
INTELLIGENCE SUMMARY

Army Form C. 2118.

Place	Date	Hour	Summary of Events and Information	Remarks and references to Appendices
BARRY	Nov 21st		Working parties as previous day. Battalion's working in two shifts. 10 Ranks to Hospital through sickness. 40 Ranks having been medically re-classified were inoculated & sent on the second half of strength.	W/O
	22nd		Working parties as usual. LT. J.F. SWINFORD, 2LTS. F.C. BAKER, G. HART. C.S. FARNBOROUGH joined the Battalion from England & were taken on strength. 40 Ranks from Hospital taken on strength.	W/O
	23rd	at 12.15	B.H.Q formed working parties as usual. Were relieved by 6 Coy. About company having been inoculated for T.A.B. 20 Ranks 15 Hospital struck off strength. 14 Ranks from Hospital taken on.	W/O
	24th		B.H.Q formed A working parties for first shift. Were relieved by B Company. 20 Ranks from Hospital taken on strength. 10 Rank & transport went inoculated. 10 Hospital struck off 20.10 of H.Q of H.O.	W/O
	25th		Working parties as usual. Specialist training. 30 Ranks from Hospital taken on. 10 Ranks to Hospital struck off.	W/O
	26th		Working parties as usual. Specialist training. NCOs classes continue. 3 Ranks to Hospital struck off. 10 Ranks from Hospital taken on.	W/O

WAR DIARY or INTELLIGENCE SUMMARY.

Army Form C. 2118.

Place	Date	Hour	Summary of Events and Information	Remarks and references to Appendices
BARRY	Nov 27th		Working Parties as usual. Work on Railway continued. Draft of 117 O.Ranks joined the Battalion from Base. Reveue taken on strength. 1 O.Rank to Hospital. 1 Officer's off.	A/W
	28th		Working Parties & Training as usual. 510 Ranks from Hospital taken on strength	A/W
	29th		Working Parties & Training. 3 O.Ranks to Hospital. 1 Officer's off. strength. 5 O.Ranks from Hospital taken on	A/W
	30th		Working Parties & Training. CAPT C. RIGDEN & 2ndLT C.E.SMITH joined the Battalion for duty. 10 Ranks to Hospital taken on strength.	A/W

C.H.Balston.
Lieut.Col.
Cmdg 6th The Buffs.

WAR DIARY
or
INTELLIGENCE SUMMARY.

Army Form C. 2118.
Sheet 1 Vol 1

MONTHLY SUMMARY.
1st to 30th November 1918

1. Administrative. During the course of the month the following officers have joined the Battalion. 2Lt C.J. PORT, F.L. HARRIS, Lt C.G. TODD, Lt J.S. SWINFORD, 2Lt F.C. BAKER, 2Lt C.S. FARMBROUGH, 2Lt G. HOKT, CAPT C. RIGDEN, 2Lt C.E. SMITH. Daft of drafts totalling 5 + 21 have joined the Battalion. Their strength was good & they brought a period of service approx 10 months. The following courses were attended during the month:-

Scouting Course	DUNSTABLE	
General "	III CORPS SCHOOL	1.0 Rank
Lewis Gun Course	ST. VALERY.	2Lt O.F. FALK 1.0 Rank
" "	III CORPS SCHOOL	CAPT J.T.H. FRIEND 1.0 Rank
NCO's		2.0 Ranks
	ETAPLES	Lt C.H. HOBSON
"	III CORPS SCHOOL	2Lt S.W. PEARNSHAW 2.0 Ranks
"	CHOCQUES	3.0 Ranks
SIGNALLING	III CORPS SCHOOL	4.0 Ranks

Army Form C. 2118.

Sheet 8
VOL.

WAR DIARY
or
INTELLIGENCE SUMMARY.
(Erase heading not required.)

Instructions regarding War Diaries and Intelligence Summaries are contained in F. S. Regs., Part II. and the Staff Manual respectively. Title pages will be prepared in manuscript.

Place	Date	Hour	Summary of Events and Information	Remarks and references to Appendices
			Courses (cont²)	
			GAS III CORPS SCHOOL LT. E.S. WILLIAMS 5.O. Ranks	
			S. OF S. PREURES. H.S. DURSTON 10 Ranks	
			P.H.B.T. OLD SCHOOL	
			COOKERY GAMACHES 1. O Rank	
			2. During the month the discipline of the Battalion has continued good throughout. He received	
			3. Morale & esprit-de-corps have seemed during the month out the health of the battalion may be called good throughout the month.	
			4. Ordnance Services Good	O.P.O.
			5. Supply " Good	
			6. Transport " Good	

WAR DIARY or INTELLIGENCE SUMMARY

Army Form C. 2118.

Sheet 9 Vol.

Place	Date	Hour	Summary of Events and Information	Remarks and references to Appendices
Operations			At HERTAIN. In the early part of the month the Battalion was in RESERVE and re-organising, holding exercises preparatory to a further advance, and inter unit & Inter Bde. TOURNAIS fifton a preliminary bombardment by the C.O. on the 8th. The Battalion was inspected by the B.G.C. on the 9th & 10th Nov who was pleased with the turnout. He disapproved of MM/S & Rofants of the Battalion, and the Battalion shoot. [unclear] ready to reach MB of the LINE in Battalion moved at 11.15 arrived at F.B. LINE at 14.45. The enemy was found to be holding the EASTERN bank of the R. SCHELDT, & a line of Resistance was consequently established along the BOULEVARD DE LEOPOLD. During the afternoon of the 9th the right 9th/9th the enemy shelled F. de LILLE lightly with H.V. shells. Our casualties were 3 killed & wounded. On the morning of 9th Patrols reported that the enemy had evacuated TOURNAI & Town was consequently taken. Reconnoitring all Bridges across the SCHELDT were found to be destroyed. On the morning 11th News was received that hostilities were to cease at 11.00. At 11.45 the Battalion moved East arriving at MONTRUEIL-aux-BOIS at 19.30, where it went into	Sheet Belgium 37 1:40,000

WAR DIARY
or
INTELLIGENCE SUMMARY.
(Erase heading not required.)

Army Form C. 2118.

Sheet No.
Vol.

Place	Date	Hour	Summary of Events and Information	Remarks and references to Appendices
	7		Operations & training (Contd)	

Preps for the night the following morning the march took was continued & the Battalion arrived at ESCANAFFLES at 1200 on the 13th. Brock on the road and inculcation & training at 1700 on the same day orders were received to move at once WEST. Subsequently the Battalion marched to HERQUEGIES went into Billets at HERQUEGIES. Further work was done on bivouacs & the Battalion worked for two hours daily until orders were received to move to BARRY. The move took place on the 14th & BARRY 1900 reached at ± 1200.

On 9th working parties were formed & work on the TOURNAI - LEUZE Railway commenced. This continued to the end of the month. Specialist & N.C.O's training was also undertaken and preparations in respect of the Police force & Labour were made.

Belgium Sheet 38. 1:100,000

Belgium Sheet 37. 1:100,000

Ypu

C H Baxton Lt Col
Comdg 10th The Buffs

WAR DIARY or INTELLIGENCE SUMMARY.

Army Form C. 2118.

Place	Date	Hour	Summary of Events and Information	Remarks and references to Appendices
BARRY	1918 Dec. 1		Battalion engaged on clearing TOURNAI-LEUZE Railway. Specialists and young N.C.O.'s training. 3 OR to Hospital struck off strength.	
"	2		Working parties and training as before.	
"	3		Holiday. Day spent in games and amusements. 1 W.O. & 6 NCO's proceeded on Tour of duty in U.K.	
"	4		Working parties and training as usual. 6 OR to Hosp. 9 OR from Base taken on Strength	
"	5		do do 6 OR to Hosp. 3 OR	
"	6		do do 3 OR do 3 OR	
"			from Base taken on strength. 2nd Lieut F.S. Kempson joined for duty and was taken on strength.	
"	7		H.M. The King visited the Division. The Bn. was drawn up on either side of the TOURNAI-LEUZE Road just outside BARRY. H.M. was enthusiastically cheered as he passed through the ranks. 5 OR to Hospital struck off strength. 10 OR from Hospital taken on strength.	
"	8		Working parties and specialist training as usual. 2 OR from Hospital taken on strength.	
"	9		Holiday. Day devoted to sports. 5 OR from Hospital taken on strength. 1 O.R. to Hospital struck off strength.	

Army Form C. 2118.

WAR DIARY
or
INTELLIGENCE SUMMARY.
(Erase heading not required.)

Instructions regarding War Diaries and Intelligence Summaries are contained in F. S. Regs., Part II. and the Staff Manual respectively. Title pages will be prepared in manuscript.

Place	Date	Hour	Summary of Events and Information	Remarks and references to Appendices
BARRY	Dec. 10		Working parties as usual. Demobilization of Miners and Pivotal men commenced. 6 OR to Base for demobilization and 1 OR to Hosp struck off strength.	
	11		Working parties as usual.	
	12		do do 4 OR from Hospital taken on strength.	
	13		do do 3 OR do	
	14		Lieut F. J. Bannock joined for duty and was taken on strength. 1 OR from Hospital taken on strength. 2 OR to Hospital struck off strength. 1 OR to Base for demobilization.	
	15		Bn. moved to FRASNES les BUISSENAL and went into billets for the night 3 OR to Hospital struck off strength.	
	16		Bn. marched on to LES DEUX ACREN and went into billets for the night 1 OR to Hospital struck off strength.	
THOLLEMBEEK	17		Bn. marched to THOLLEMBEEK arriving at midday and went into Billets	
	18		Training commenced. 1 OR to Hospital struck off strength.	
	19		Owing to insufficient billeting accommodation at THOLLEMBEEK 'A' and 'C' Coys. moved to VOLLEZEEL (neighbouring village) and were billeted there. 15 OR from Hospital taken on strength. 6 OR to Hospital struck off rations 1 OR to Base for demobilization.	

Army Form C. 2118.

WAR DIARY
or
INTELLIGENCE SUMMARY.
(Erase heading not required.)

Instructions regarding War Diaries and Intelligence Summaries are contained in F. S. Regs., Part II. and the Staff Manual respectively. Title pages will be prepared in manuscript.

Place	Date	Hour	Summary of Events and Information	Remarks and references to Appendices
THOLLEMBEEK	Dec 20		Training as usual. 1 OR to Base for demobilization. 5 OR from Base taken on strength.	
"	21		Training as usual.	
"	22		Training as usual. 1 OR from Base taken on strength. 1 OR to Hosp struck off strength.	
"	23		Training as usual.	
"	24		Training as usual.	
"	25		Holiday	
"	26		do. 8 OR draft taken on strength. 7 OR from Hosp taken on strength. 1 OR to Base for demobilization struck off strength.	
"	27		Training as usual. 1 OR from Hospital taken on strength. 2 OR to Hospital struck off strength. 1 OR to Base for demobilization struck off strength.	
"	28		Training as usual. All OR were classified and grouped for Educational purposes.	
"	29		Training as usual. 1 OR to Hosp struck off strength. 2 OR from Hospital taken on strength.	
"	30		Training as usual. 1 OR to Hosp. and 2 OR to Base for demobilization struck off strength. 24 OR from Base taken on strength.	
"	31		Training as usual. 2 OR to Hospital struck off strength.	

C H Balston Lt Col
Commanding 10th The Buffs

WAR DIARY
or
INTELLIGENCE SUMMARY.
(Erase heading not required.)

Army Form C. 2118.

Place	Date	Hour	Summary of Events and Information	Remarks and references to Appendices
	1918 Dec.		<u>Administration</u> During the course of the month the following Officers have joined the Bn:- 2nd Lieut. F.S. Kempson, Lieut. F.J. Bannock 2 drafts of O.R. joined the Bn. totalling 32. Their physique was good and their average period of service 2½ years. The following courses were attended during the month. <table><tr><td>Course</td><td>Place</td><td>Officers</td><td>Other Ranks</td></tr><tr><td>Cookery</td><td>III Corps school.</td><td>-</td><td>1</td></tr><tr><td>Sniping</td><td>1st Army School</td><td>-</td><td>6</td></tr><tr><td>Agriculture</td><td>Lille</td><td>-</td><td>3</td></tr><tr><td>Musketry</td><td>MATRINGHEM</td><td>-</td><td>4</td></tr><tr><td>Education</td><td>OXFORD</td><td>Lt E.S. Williams</td><td>-</td></tr></table> <u>Discipline</u> The discipline of the Bn. continued good throughout the month.	

Army Form C. 2118.

WAR DIARY
or
INTELLIGENCE SUMMARY.
(Erase heading not required.)

Place	Date	Hour	Summary of Events and Information	Remarks and references to Appendices
	1918 Dec		Health The health of the Bn. has been good during the month. No cases of infectious disease seen reported.	
			Ordnance Services — Good.	
			Supply — do — Indifferent.	
			Transport — do — Good.	

C.H. Baldwin
Lieut - Colonel
Commanding 10th The Buffs.

10th The Buffs

Army Form C. 2118.

Jan 1919
SHEET 1

WAR DIARY
INTELLIGENCE SUMMARY
(Erase heading not required.)

Instructions regarding War Diaries and Intelligence Summaries are contained in F.S. Regs., Part II. and the Staff Manual respectively. Title pages will be prepared in manuscript.

Place	Date	Hour	Summary of Events and Information	Remarks and references to Appendices
THOLLEMBEEK BELGIUM	1st Jan 1919		Company inspections, training and education. Capt. D.S. CAMPBELL, M.C. was appointed A.D.C. to 3rd CORPS COMD and was struck off the strength. 2 O.R. to Hospital and struck off the strength.	Ref. map BELGIUM 1:40.000 EDITION II
	2.		Company Inspections. P.T. & Arms drill & Education. 74 "Div Cinema" closed at VOLLEZEL. Major C.E. PONSONBY returned from Senior Officers Course in U.K. and resumed duties of 2nd in command. 1 O.R. to hospital and struck off the strength. 2. O.R. to Base for duty and struck off the strength.	
	3.		Company Inspections. P.T. Arms Drill, Education, football. 9 O.R. from Base taken on the strength.	
	4.		2 Companies route march, remainder Education. 6 O.R. proceeded to Base for Demobilisation. 1 O.R. from hospital taken on strength. 1 O.R. to hospital struck off the strength.	

WAR DIARY or INTELLIGENCE SUMMARY

Army Form C. 2118.

SHEET. 2.

Place	Date	Hour	Summary of Events and Information	Remarks and references to Appendices
THOLLEMBEEK'S	Jan 1919.		Coy Inspections, P.T. & Arms drill, Education. Football	REF. MAP BELGIUM 1:40,000. EDITION II
BELGIUM.	5th		1 Coy v 230th F.A. at GAMMARAGES. Capt. J.I.H. FRIEND M.C. & 7 O.R. to Base for Demobilization and struck off the strength.	
	6.		Coy Inspections. P.T. & Arms Drill. Coy League football in afternoon. 3. O.R. from Hospital taken on the strength. 1.O.R. to Base for Demobilization struck off the strength. The Church Army Canteen was opened at THOLLEMBEEK.	
	7.		Coy Inspections, Education. Football. 10 Yth Buffs v 231 Brigade H.Q. in Semi final for Div Cup. 7. O.R. proceeded to Base for transfer to U.K. 2. O.R. to Hospital and were struck off the strength.	
	8.		P. T. R.T. & Arms drill. Inter Coy League football. 3. O.R. from Base taken on the strength.	
	9.		2 Coys Route march. Remainder Education. Football Inter Units Div Cup Competition. 10. O.R. proceeded to Base two	

Army Form C. 2118.

SHEET 3.

WAR DIARY
INTELLIGENCE SUMMARY.
(Erase heading not required.)

Place	Date	Hour	Summary of Events and Information	Remarks and references to Appendices
THOLLEMBEEK, BELGIUM.	Jan 9. (contd)		for Demobilization and 2.O.R. to Hospital. Struck off the strength.	REF MAP. BELGIUM. 1:40,000 EDITION II.
	10.		Coy inspections and Arms drill. Football. one 2 Coys route march remainder education. 1.O.R to hospital, struck off the strength. 2.O.R. from hospital taken on the strength.	
	11.			
	12		22 O.R. proceeded to Base for demobilization and were struck off the strength.	
	13.		Coy inspections. P. & R.T. & Arms drill. Education. Football. 1/c H.S. DURSTON and 14 O.R. proceeded to Base for demobilization and were struck off the strength.	
	14.		Coy inspections. Education. 1.O.R. to hospital, struck off the strength. 3.O.R. from Base taken on the strength.	

Army Form C. 2118.

SHEET 4.

WAR DIARY
or
INTELLIGENCE SUMMARY.
(Erase heading not required.)

Instructions regarding War Diaries and Intelligence Summaries are contained in F. S. Regs., Part II. and the Staff Manual respectively. Title pages will be prepared in manuscript.

Place	Date	Hour	Summary of Events and Information	Remarks and references to Appendices
THOLLEMBEEK BELGIUM.	Jan. 15.		Coy inspections. P. + R.T. and Arms drill. Education. 14 O.R. proceeded to Base for demobilization, struck off the strength. 1. O.R. joined as draft, taken on strength.	REF MAP. BELGIUM 1:40.000 EDITION II
	16	7a	Coy inspections. P. + R.T. 25 O.R. proceeded to Base for demobilization. 2. O.R. to Hospital struck off the strength. 1. O.R. from Leave, 2. O.R from hosp., 2. O.R. from Leave 1 O.R. from course taken on the strength.	
	17.		Coy inspections. P. + R.T. and Arms drill. Education. 1. O.R. rejoined from hospital, 7. O.R. rejoined from 230th L.T.M.B. 3. O.R. rejoined from 230th Brigade H.Q. 1. O.R. ex Leave taken on the strength.	
	18.		Coy inspections and Arms drill. 2. O.R. proceeded to Base for demobilization. LT. COL. C. H. BALSTON and 1. O.R. proceeded on leave to U.K. Football 10th Yks Buffs V. 10th K.S.L.I.	

WAR DIARY
INTELLIGENCE SUMMARY.

Army Form C. 2118.

SHEET. 5

Place	Date	Hour	Summary of Events and Information	Remarks and references to Appendices
THOLLEMBEEK BELGIUM.	Jan 19th		Church Parade at THOLLEMBEEK and VOLLEZEEL. 2.O.R. to hospital, 12.O.R proceeded to Base for demobilization, and struck off the strength. 2.O.R. reporting from hospital and were taken on the strength.	REF. MAP. BELGIUM. 1/40,000. EDITION II
	20.		Training. 14.O.R. proceeded to Base for demobilization struck off the strength. 1.O.R. from hospital taken on the strength.	
	21.		Preliminary inspection at THOLLEMBEEK and VOLLEZEEL preparatory to Royal Inspection at BRUSSELS. H.Q and 2 Coys bathing. 1.O.R. to hospital struck off the strength. 1.O.R. from Base and 1.O.R. from leave in U.K. taken on the strength.	
	22.		Training under Coy arrangements. 12.O.R. proceeded to Base for demobilization, struck off the strength. 1.O.R. rejoined from hospital taken on the strength.	

WAR DIARY or INTELLIGENCE SUMMARY

Army Form C. 2118.

SHEET 6

Place	Date	Hour	Summary of Events and Information	Remarks and references to Appendices
THOLLEMBEEK BELGIUM.	Jan. 23		Batt. was inspected at VOLLEZEEL by B.G.C. 74th Div. composite Brigade, prior to Royal Inspection at BRUSSELS by H.M. KING ALBERT. 1.O.R. returned from Course 2.O.R. from Base taken on the strength. 2.O.R. proceeded to Base for demobilization and 1.O.R. proceeded on leave to U.K. and were struck off the strength. one Training under Coy arrangements. one	REF MAP BELGIUM. 1:40.000. EDITION II
	24			
	25		Battalion entrussed at VOLLEZEEL at 0900. At midday Battalion arrived at ANDERLECHT (BRUSSELS) and went into billets. Remainder of the day was spent in preparing for the march past on the following day.	REF MAP BELGIUM. BRUSSELS 1:100,000 EDITION II
BRUSSELS.	26		Battalion paraded at 0930 and marched through BRUSSELS towards the PALAIS DU ROI, passing the saluting base at 1200. The salute was taken by H.M. the King of the Belgians. The march past being	

WAR DIARY
or
INTELLIGENCE SUMMARY.
(Erase heading not required.)

Army Form C. 2118.

SHEET 7.

Place	Date	Hour	Summary of Events and Information	Remarks and references to Appendices
BRUSSELS.	Jan 26. (contd)		much appreciated by the population of the City. Battalion arrived back in billeting area at 14.30. Remainder of the day was spent as a holiday. The day was regarded as a holiday throughout the Battalion.	REF. MAP. BELGIUM. BRUSSELS. 1:100,000 EDITION II.
	27.			
	28.		Battalion embussed at 1000, arriving back at VOLLEZEEL at 14.30.	
THOLLEMBEEK	29.		Training. P.T., R.T. Education. 2 O.R. returned from Courses, taken on the strength.	REF. MAP. BELGIUM 1:40,000 EDITION II.
	30.		Training as usual. 1 O.R. to hospital, struck off the strength. 1 O.R. from Base taken on the strength.	
			Training as usual. 1 O.R. on Emigration Leave. 2 O.R. to Hospital struck off the strength.	

[Stamp: 3rd R. KENT REGD. BATTn THE BUFFS * ORDERLY ROOM * No. / Date 1/2/19]

Connolly Major
Cmdg 10th The Buffs.

Army Form C. 2118.

SHEET I

WAR DIARY
or
INTELLIGENCE SUMMARY.
(Erase heading not required.)

Place	Date	Hour	Summary of Events and Information	Remarks, and references to Appendices
			Summary.	
			from 1st to 31st Jan. 1919.	
			1. Administrative	
			During the course of the month 8 off and 200 O.R. have proceeded to Base for demobilization. 2 drafts have joined the Battalion. The following Courses were attended.	
			Course. Officers O.R.	
			Armourers. - 2.	
			Suit growing - 3.	
			At. CALAIS. NORBECOURT - 1 10th Bde. R.A.F. -	
			2. Health.	
			During the course of the month, the health of the Battalion has been good. 2 cases of mumps only have been reported.	

Army Form C. 2118.

SHEET II

WAR DIARY
or
INTELLIGENCE SUMMARY.
(Erase heading not required.)

Place	Date	Hour	Summary of Events and Information	Remarks and references to Appendices
			3. Ordnance. Services, good.	
			4. Supply. Services, indifferent.	
			5. Transport. Services, good.	
			6. Training:- During the month Recreational, Educational, and Military training has been in progress. Inter Coy Inter Section Sports such as Football, and Country Runs etc has been undertaken. On the 21st the O/13.B.G.C. inspected the Battalion preparatory to the Royal Inspection at BRUSSELS. The Battalion was again inspected by the 13.B.C. Comdg. 74"(Yeo) Division Composite Brigade on the 23rd. On the 25" the Battalion embussed at VOLLEZEEL at midday, going into billets at BRUSSELS at ANDERLECHT. and arrived at BRUSSELS	REF.MAP. BELGIUM SHEET 30. 1:40.000 EDITION. II.

WAR DIARY
INTELLIGENCE SUMMARY
(Erase heading not required.)

Army Form C. 2118.

SHEET III

The Battalion paraded at 0930 on Sunday 26th and proceeded towards the Palais du Roi, where it marched past the Saluting Base, the salute being taken by H.M. King Albert. The following day was regarded as a holiday and was much appreciated by all ranks. On the 28th the Battalion entrained at 1000 and returned to VOLLEZEEL and THOLLEMBEEK.

Cranley Major.
Cmdg. 10 THE BUFFS.

Army Form C. 2118.

Sheet 1.
10 Batt Essex Regts
Lt Col ??

WAR DIARY
or
INTELLIGENCE SUMMARY.
(Erase heading not required.)

Map Belgium. Sheet 30. & II
1:40000   W 30 6
33

Place	Date	Hour	Summary of Events and Information	Remarks and references to Appendices
Chatelineck Belgium	1919 Oct 1		P. & O. Arms Drill. Lecture at Volleyeel by 2/Lt. Earnshaws. Subject "money".	
	2		Church Service at Volleyeel & Shollombeek. 2 Officers & 25 OR proceeded to the Base for 5 min St. & were struck off strength.	
	3		P. & R. & Arms Drill. Education & Lectures. 13 O.R. proceeded to Base for 5 min St. & were struck off strength.	
	4		P. & R. & Arms Drill. There was a Batt Cross Country run to pick team for Divnl run. Ammunition pots were worn by all ranks taking part. 1 man to 5 A.	
	5		P. R. & Arms Drill. Education & Lectures. at 14.15 there was a final Cross Country run to select team for Divn. Comp.	
	6		P. & R. Arms Drill. Football en	
	7		Coy Supee etc. Football 1 Off. & 12 O.R. proceeded to Base for 5 min St. & were struck off the strength. Capt & adj.	
	8		W. Stanley	

WAR DIARY
or
INTELLIGENCE SUMMARY.
(Erase heading not required.)

Army Form C. 2118.

Sheet 2

Place	Date	Hour	Summary of Events and Information	Remarks and references to Appendices
Watten, Belgium	Feb 8.		2/R.W.F. Arms Drill Football etc. 2/Lt Watts & Lt. A.Y.S. Thornton proceeded to Base for Demob. Were Struck off Strength. 1OR rejoined from Hosp. Taken on strength. Batt HQ. moved to Wulleghem from Dhollowbeck. for Admin Rations A & C Coys were amalgamated & known as A & C Coy.	Place 30 X 7 c 8.5
	9.		Church Services. Batt HQ coy dissolved & Tpd to A & C Coys. 1 Off. 9 OR (Ples Harris) proceeded to Base in Wulleghem. Div. Cinema at Wulleghem.	II B
	10.		2/R.W.F. Arms Drill Lecture by Col. DR Barnhurst Goodwin of the 7th Welsh on Bayonets. 2OR rejoined from Base to France. Capt C Rigden & Lt C.S. Yarnborough and 10 OR. Prov. to Base for Demob & were taken on strength for purpose of Admin in Cos & were amalgamated. The Divl Cross Country Run took place at Rosières. The result was (1) 4 RW (2) 10 RW (3) 9 RWF

WAR DIARY
or
INTELLIGENCE SUMMARY.
(Erase heading not required.)

Army Form C. 2118.

Sheet 3

Place	Date	Hour	Summary of Events and Information	Remarks and references to Appendices
	Feb 11		Coy Duties and Arms Drill. Football. Education	
	12		Coy Duties. Arms Drill. Lecture by Capt Clarke (Manic type) and Arms Drill. Football. Education. Discussions	
	13		Coy Duties and Arms Drill. The 16th Sussex Concert Party should visit Meergeel 2OR to Hosp. 2OR to Base for unfit. Strength 88. Strength.	
	14			
	15		POR 1. 16 Sussex Concert Party at Cheltenham. 90R rejoined from 230. 4 NCO Others on strength 4 OR proceeded to Base for demob. Struck off strength	
	16	10 RMS	Church services. III Corps Cross Country Run, the Bn and furnishes and sal. 2 Off & 20 OR represented. the Bn. ab of 18 other teams from Hosp. Taken on strength. 10R demob on leave It. M.B. Wade proceeded to join 173. Inft. Capt Dickenson from Letach all struck off strength	II 30 1.4.88.09 Struck off
	17		POR 1. Football. Lectures. POR. rej from Base. Taken on strength - Struck off strength	2/4

WAR DIARY or INTELLIGENCE SUMMARY.

Army Form C. 2118.
Sheet 4

Place	Date 1919	Hour	Summary of Events and Information	Remarks and references to Appendices
Calais, Belgium	Sept 18		Coy Inspec. & Arms Drill. Bathing. Football & education. 2/Lt Kempson proceeded to UK on 14 days leave	
	19		Coy Inspec & Arms Drill. Football AC/335 Corp Resvd S-for B.5	
	20		Coy Inspec. Bathing. 6 OR proceeded to Base for Demob.	
	21		P.J.R.J. Lectures & football. Lt for Berkhamstead to Capt Adjt 3 OR to Base for Demob.	
	22		Coy Inspec. 1 OR from Base taken on strength. 6 OR to Base for Demob. Church Strength 2 Officers on Draft Cond Nd to UK.	
	23		Church Service. 2/Lt J. Smith proceeded on Draft Cond Duty. 1 OR rejoined from Hosp. taken on strength. 16 OR proceeded to Base for Demob. Church off strength.	
Calais, Belgium	24		53 OR to Base for Demob.	
	25		P.J.R.J. 1 OR from Hosp. taken on strength.	

Army Form C. 2118.
Sept 30
1:40,000
Ed 3
1/X

2353 Wt. W2544/1454 700,000 5/15 D. D. & L. A.D.S.S./Forms/C. 2118.

WAR DIARY
or
INTELLIGENCE SUMMARY.

Army Form C. 2118.

Sheet 5.

Place	Date	Hour	Summary of Events and Information	Remarks and references to Appendices
Vollezel Belgium	1919 Feb 26		10 Inspec. 1 OR from Base taken on strength	Belgium Sheet-30
Frammont Belgium	27		Moved to Frammont. A farewell address was handed to the Burgomasters of Vollegel & Thielenbeek thanking the inhabitants of each village for their hospitality during our stay. The Battalion left amid popular demonstrations 3 of pct. 1 57 OR proceeded to Base for Demob.	1/40000 Sheet II
	28		Day spent cleaning & clearing the chateau in which Battalion is billeted. 1 OR rejoined from Hospital taken on strength.	

Crombey Major
Commanding 10 The Buffs.

WAR DIARY or INTELLIGENCE SUMMARY

Army Form C. 2118.

Sheet 1.

Place	Date	Hour	Summary of Events and Information	Remarks and references to Appendices
			1 Administrative. During the month 8 Officers & 281 OR proceeded to Base for dem & 2 other Officers struck off strength. No drafts joined the Battalion. The following courses were attended.	
			24459. Pte Tain C Course of Instruction.	
			2 Health Good	
			3 Ordnance Services Good	
			4 Supply Services Fair	
			5 Transport Services Good	
			6 Training. During the month Recreational & Educational Sports training have been in progress, but owing to the very inclement weather generally prevailing sports games etc have been somewhat curtailed. The Batt. was 3rd in the Div two Country Run near Bosines and 5th out of 18 when they represented the Div in the Corps two Country Run	

Army Form C. 2118.

WAR DIARY
or
INTELLIGENCE SUMMARY.

Sheet 2

(Erase heading not required)

Instructions regarding War Diaries and Intelligence Summaries are contained in F. S. Regs., Part II. and the Staff Manual respectively. Title pages will be prepared in manuscript.

Place	Date	Hour	Summary of Events and Information	Remarks and references to Appendices
		6	Training cont'd. At Nal'il the Batt'n (except parts (Ali Blotto) completed training and earned high praise for their performances. Friendly relations of an exceptional character were established between the Batt'n and the inhabitants of Nalleged & Thollombeeh and the Batt'n left amid demonstrations of regret.	

C.H.H. by Major.
Commanding 10 The Buffs.

Army Form C. 2118.
10th The Buffs
MARCH 1919

Sheet I. 12

WAR DIARY
or
INTELLIGENCE SUMMARY.
(Erase heading not required.)

Place	Date	Hour	Summary of Events and Information	Remarks and references to Appendices
GRAMMONT	MARCH 1.		For the purpose of administration. A.C. Coy and B.D. Coy were amalgamated as one Coy under the command of 2/Lt C.E. Smith. 2 O.R. from Hospital were taken on the strength.	Map Ref. BELGIUM. Sheet 30. Ed. II. 1:40,000. V.2.b. S.S.
	2.		Church Services were held in the Y.M.C.A. GRAMMONT.	
	3.		The C.O. regrets to announce the sudden death, from natural causes, of 21817 Pte E.C. Tucker. On this date our first batch of animals proceeded for demobilization. (9 horses & 7 mules. I.O.R. to T.A. struck off the strength.	
	4.		Football and Arms drill.	
	5.		Funeral of the late Pte E.S. Tucker. Full Military Honours were observed. 4 more horses proceeded to Base for Demob.	
	6.		The day was spent chiefly in refitting the 1916 Class men, who are proceeding to join the Army of Occupation. The C.O. had much pleasure in presenting the Military Medal to 9927 W.S.M. English and to 271039 Pte Hinton, for gallantry in the field.	56 23

Army Form C. 2118.

WAR DIARY
or
INTELLIGENCE SUMMARY.

(Erase heading not required.)

Sheet No. 2.

Place	Date	Hour	Summary of Events and Information	Remarks and references to Appendices
GRAMMONT	Mar. 7		2 Lt Gulley, 2 Lt R.M. Wright, 4 R.S.M. Dray and a draft of 109 O.R. proceeded to HARVE to join the 1st Bn of the Royal West Surrey Regt. 3. O.R. proceeded to LILLE for duty. 2 O.R. returned from Draft conditg duty to U.K.	MAP. BELGIUM. Sheet 30 Ed. II. 1:40,000. V. 2. b. 5. 5.
	8		The Bn. now about 96 strong, everybody being employed on cleaning or in Q.M. Stores. Lewis guns etc being oiled and packed in readiness for embarkation to U.K. 1. O.R. to Hosp.	
	9		Church Services.	
	10		Everybody employed. 2 Lt Pott & 2 Lt Hampson returned from leave in U.K.	
	11		Usual Routine. 5 mules evacuated for sale locally.	
	12		" " 4 " " " "	
	13		Major C.E. Bowsorby assumes the rank of Lt. Col. 1 Horse to Ph. Base for Repatriation.	

Army Form C. 2118.

WAR DIARY
or
INTELLIGENCE SUMMARY.
(Erase heading not required.)

Sheet III

Place	Date	Hour	Summary of Events and Information	Remarks and references to Appendices
GRAMMONT	Feb/14		Everybody employed in clearing up the grounds of the Chateau.	MAP. BELGIUM. Sheet 30. E. II 1:40.000. V.26. S.S.
	15.		St. Todd and 2.O.R. to the Base for demobilization.	
	16.		Church Services in Garrison. 1 Riding horse proceeded for Demob.	
	17.		2.O.R. from Hosp. 1.O.R. evacuated to Hospital.	
	18.		Officers and men spending their spare time in gardening in the grounds of the Chateau. 2 Riding horses proceeded to ATH. for sale locally.	
	19.		Gardening etc. 2.O.R. to Base for Demobilization.	
	20.		Usual Routine, Gardening etc.	
	21.		Lt Swinford retired from detachment as Sub Area Commandant	
OLIGNIES.			The Rev. A. Roughley, the Wesleyan Chaplain attached	

Army Form C. 2118.

WAR DIARY
or
INTELLIGENCE SUMMARY.
(Erase heading not required.)

Sheet IV

Place	Date	Hour	Summary of Events and Information	Remarks and references to Appendices
GRAMMONT.	Jan. 21 cont.		to this Unit, proceeded to No 4 Stationary Hospital.	MAP.
			ST. OMER for duty.	BELGIUM. Sheet 30.
	22.		The Bn moved from the Chateau to the Eastern end of	Ed. II.
			the town, into more comfortable billets. Capt. H. g. Hollborn	1:40,000.
			rejoined from leave in the U.K.	V. 2. b.
	23.		Church Services. 2.O.R. to Hospital.	5. 5.
	24.		15. O.R. to Base for Demobilization. Bn now down to Cadre strength in readiness for embarkation to U.K.	
	25.		Usual Routine.	
	26.		Usual Routine.	
	27.		6.O.R. to Base for demobilization.	
			Football. First Round of Divisional "Cadre"	
	28.		Knockout. 10th The Buffs v. 15 Suffolk Regt. The Buffs	
			won by 2 goals.	

Army Form C. 2118.

WAR DIARY
or
INTELLIGENCE SUMMARY.
(Erase heading not required.)

Sheet V

Place	Date	Hour	Summary of Events and Information	Remarks and references to Appendices
GRAMMONT.	29th		Usual Routine	MAP. BELGIUM Sheet 30. I.D.II 1:40.000. V.2.b. S.S.
	30.		Church Services	
	31.		Gymkana held by the 229th Brigade. 4 O.R. (1916 Class) proceeded to join 1st Bn. Royal West Surrey Regt. Capt. C.E. Smith, 2Lt. G. Haughton and 3 O.R. proceeded to the Base for Demob.	

Oliver Lt. Col.
Commanding 10th The Buffs.

WAR DIARY
or
INTELLIGENCE SUMMARY.
(Erase heading not required.)

Army Form C. 2118.

Sheet 1.

Place	Date	Hour	Summary of Events and Information	Remarks and references to Appendices
			Summary. During the month the Battn. has been reduced to "Cadre" Strength preparatory to leaving for U.K. All the retainable class Men left as a draft for the 1st Royal West Surrey Regt. with the Army of Occupation. The remainder of the eligible men have been demobilized. No training has been carried out, the Cadre of the Battn. have been engaged on work with the Transport and Stores. Recreation, such as football has been limited, a few afternoons during each week being all that has been possible.	

Army Form C. 2118.

WAR DIARY
or
INTELLIGENCE SUMMARY.
(Erase heading not required.)

Sheet II.

Place	Date	Hour	Summary of Events and Information	Remarks and references to Appendices

1. Administration. During the course of the month 4 Offrs & 35 O.R. have proceeded to the Base for Draft. 2 Offrs & 110 O.R. proceeded to join 1st Royal West Surrey Regt as a draft.

2. Health. The health of the Batt. has been good.

3. Ordnance Service. Good.
4. Supply. Fair.
5. Transport. Good.

6. Training. No training has been carried out.

Crumly Lt Col.
Cmdg 10th yb Buffs.

Army Form C. 2118.

"10 E Kent Q"

Sheet I/B

WAR DIARY
or
INTELLIGENCE SUMMARY.
(Erase heading not required.)

Instructions regarding War Diaries and Intelligence Summaries are contained in F. S. Regs., Part II and the Staff Manual respectively. Title pages will be prepared in manuscript.

Place	Date	Hour	Summary of Events and Information	Remarks and references to Appendices
GRAMMONT	April.			Map Belgium Sheet 30. Edition II 1:40.000 V.2. G.55.
	1.		At Grammont. The Cadre all employed oiling and cleaning stores. Football in afternoon.	
	2.		Usual Routine. Football.	
	3.		" "	
	4.		" " Captain Hollebone, Peel & Barnard proceeded to the Base for Demobilisation.	
	5.		Usual Routine. Football in afternoon.	
	6.		Church Services. Football 2nd Round of Divisional Cadre 10th Bn. Buffs v. 26th R.W.F. Result Buffs 3 goals. R.W.F. 1 goal.	
	7.		Usual Routine.	
	8.		Usual Routine. Semi-final of Div. Cadre football competition 10th Bn. Buffs v. 229th F. Amb. Result no goals scored.	
	9.		Usual Routine. In afternoon replay of Semi-final. Result 10th Bn. Buffs 0 229th F. Amb. 1. Capt. D.S. Francis proceeded to the Base for Demob.	96 24

Army Form C. 2118.

WAR DIARY
or
INTELLIGENCE SUMMARY.
(Erase heading not required.)

Sheet II

Place	Date	Hour	Summary of Events and Information	Remarks and references to Appendices
GRAMMONT	April 10.		Usual Routine. Capt G. A. Pecklan proceeded on 14 days leave to the U.K.	Map BELGIUM. Sheet 30. Ed. II. 1:40,000 V.2, 6, S.S.
	11.		Usual Routine.	
	12.		"	
	13.		Church Services. Football in afternoon.	
	14.		Usual Routine. 2nd Lts J. L. Lilley & Y. C. Baker proceeded to the Base for Demobilization.	
	15.		Usual Routine. Lts G. S. Downs & Kempson, 2Lts Swinford, Hart, G. Smith, G. J. Pool G. proceeded for duty with Prisoners of War Coys.	
	16.		Usual Routine. 1. O. R. proceeded to form the 1st Bn. the Royal West Surrey Regt.	
	17.		Usual Routine. 2 O. R. returned from duty at 5th Army H.Q.	
	18.		Usual Routine.	

Army Form C. 2118.

WAR DIARY
or
INTELLIGENCE SUMMARY.
(Erase heading not required.)

Sheet III.

Place	Date	Hour	Summary of Events and Information	Remarks and references to Appendices
GRAMMONT	April.			Map.
	19th		Usual Routine. Football Etc.	BELGIUM.
	20.		Church Services.	Sheet 20.
	21.		Easter Monday.	Ed. II.
			Holiday. Sports observed throughout the Division as an	1:40000.
			holiday. Short lecture by the C.O. in afternoon. 4.O.R. proceeded	V. 2.
			to the U.K. for leave.	6. S.S.
	22.		Usual Routine. Lt.Col. C. Ponsonby proceeded on 14 days	
			leave to the U.K.	
	23.		Usual Routine. 2.O.R. proceeded to join the 1st R.W. Survey.	
	24.		" " 1 " " " "	
	25.		" " our last batch of animals & mules evacuated.	
	26.		" "	
	27.		Church Services. Capt. G.H. Peckham rejoined from leave	
			in the U.K.	
	28.		Usual Routine. 1.O.R. to the Base for Demob.	

Army Form C. 2118.

WAR DIARY
or
INTELLIGENCE SUMMARY.
(Erase heading not required.)

Place	Date	Hour	Summary of Events and Information	Remarks and references to Appendices
GRAMMONT	April 29.		Usual Routine.	Map. Belgium. Sheet 30 Ed. II. 1/40,000. V. 2, 6, S.5.
	30.		"	

Signature
Captain & Adj't
O.C. 10th Yorks Buff.

Army Form C. 2118.

WAR DIARY
or
INTELLIGENCE SUMMARY.
(Erase heading not required.)

Sheet I.

Place	Date	Hour	Summary of Events and Information	Remarks and references to Appendices
			Summary:- The Battalion has been at Cadre Strength the whole of the past month. All eligible men returning to the Unit have been demobilized, all obtainable 1916 Class returning have been drafted to the 1st Batn. the Royal West Surrey Regt. There has been a certain amount of football. The Battalion XI won its way to the semi-final of the Divisional Competition, but at that point were beaten by the "229th" F.A.

1. Administrative. During the course of the month 6 O.F.F. & 8 O.R. proceeded to the Base for Demob. 7. O.R. were drafted to the "Surreys". 6 Officers (Volunteers for Army of Occupation) proceeded for duty with various P. of War Coys. | |

Army Form C. 2118.

WAR DIARY
or
INTELLIGENCE SUMMARY.   Sheet II.
(Erase heading not required.)

Place	Date	Hour	Summary of Events and Information	Remarks and references to Appendices

Summary

(2) Health. The health of the Battⁿ has been very good.

(3) Ordnance Service "

(4) Supply "

(5) Training. No training has been carried out.

(6) Discipline. The discipline of the Battⁿ has been excellent.

Capt. & Adjt.
O.C. 10th E. Buffs.

WAR DIARY or INTELLIGENCE SUMMARY

Army Form C. 2118.

10 E Kent Fs

Sheet I.

Place	Date	Hour	Summary of Events and Information	Remarks and references to Appendices
GRAMMONT	MAY 1.		The "Cadre still" at GRAMMONT. Usual Routine. 1 OR to U.K for leave.	MAP BELGIUM 1:40,000. Sheet 30. ED II. V.2.b.5.5.
	2.		Usual Routine. Capt. K. G. Hollebone (now Demobilized) to be A/Major from 18/1/19.	
	3.		Usual Routine. 1 OR from Base taken on the strength.	
	4.		Church Services. 1 OR to the U.K for leave.	
	5.		Usual Routine.	
	6.	"	230th Bde Whist Drive in Evening. 2 OR to U.K for leave.	
	7.	"	2 OR (returnable) proceeded as a draft to join the 1 Bn Royal West Surrey Regt. 1 OR to the U.K. for leave.	
	8.	"	1 OR to Base for demobilization.	
	9.	"		
	10.		Cricket in afternoon.	
	11.		Church Services. 1 OR to Hospital.	
	12.		Lt Col. C.E. Pennaly rejoined from leave to the U.K. Cricket in afternoon. 230th Inf Bde. V. 242 Bde R.F.A. (Result 230th Bde won by 11 runs)	f. 25.

Army Form C. 2118.

WAR DIARY
or
INTELLIGENCE SUMMARY.
(Erase heading not required.)

Sheet II.

Place: GRAMMONT

Date	Hour	Summary of Events and Information	Remarks and references to Appendices
May 13.		Usual Routine. Artillery Sports in afternoon.	MAP BELGIUM. 1:40,000. Sheet 30. Ed II. V.2.4.&5.
14		" " Cricket Practice in afternoon.	
15.		" "	
16.		All day cricket match 230th Inf Bde v. 242 Army Bde R.F.A. 230th Bde won by 40 runs.	
17.		Usual Routine.	
18.		" "	
19.		Church Services. Cricket in Afternoon.	
20		Lt. Col. C.E. Pennerby proceeded on 14 days leave to the U.K.	
21.		" "	
22		" "	
23		" "	
24		C o.B. proceeded on leave to the U.K.	
25.		Church Services.	
26		Usual Routine.	

Army Form C. 2118.

WAR DIARY
or
INTELLIGENCE SUMMARY.
(Erase heading not required.)

Sheet III.

Place	Date	Hour	Summary of Events and Information	Remarks and references to Appendices
GRAMMONT	May 27.		Usual Routine	MAP BELGIUM 1/40.000. Sheet 30. Ed II. V.2.6.5.5.
	28.		A further reduction of the Cadre Battals. ordered. 7. ORs to Base for Demobilisation	
	29.		Usual Routine. 1 OR to Hospital	
	30.		"	
	31.		All day Cricket Match. 220th Inf Bde v. 242 Bde R.F.A. won for the R.F.A. by 8 wickets.	

R. Parker Capt.
O.C. 10th G.R. Buffs.

Army Form C. 2118.

WAR DIARY
or
INTELLIGENCE SUMMARY.

(Erase heading not required.)

Sheet 1.

Place	Date	Hour	Summary of Events and Information	Remarks and references to Appendices
GRAMMONT	MAY.		Summary:- During the past month there has been a further reduction in the Cadre Establishment of the Bn., our effective strength now being 4 Officers and about 40 OR. No training has been carried out. There has been a certain amount of sports, mainly Cricket. 1. Administration. During the course of the month 10 ORs proceeded to the Base for Demobilization. 2 ORs proceeded to join the Royal West Surrey Regt. (reservists). 2. Health. The health of the "Cadre" has been excellent.	MAP. BELGIUM. 1:40,000. Sheet 30. 50.II. V.2.u.5.5.

WAR DIARY
or
INTELLIGENCE SUMMARY.

(Erase heading not required.)

Army Form C. 2118.

Sheet II.

Place	Date	Hour	Summary of Events and Information	Remarks and references to Appendices
GRAMMONT	MAY		Summary contd.	MAP BELGIUM. 1:40,000. Ed II. Sheet 30. V.a.2.5.5
			3. Ordnance Services. Good.	
			4. Supply " Poor.	
			5. Discipline. The discipline of the Cadre has been excellent.	

Durham
Capt.
O.C. 10th Offr. 1 Buffs.

www.ingramcontent.com/pod-product-compliance
Lightning Source LLC
Chambersburg PA
CBHW081438160426
43193CB00013B/2316